Worlds of Talk

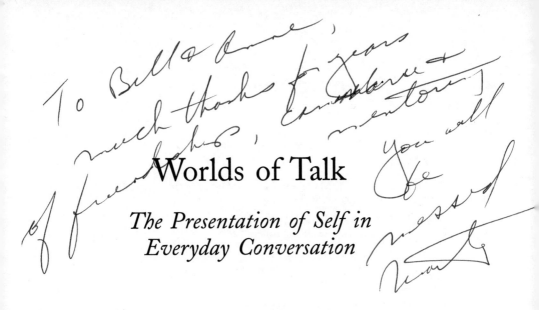

Worlds of Talk

The Presentation of Self in Everyday Conversation

MARTIN J. MALONE

Polity Press

Copyright © Martin J. Malone 1997

The right of Martin J. Malone to be identified as author of this work has been asserted in accordance with the Copyright, Designs and Patents Act 1988.

First published in 1997 by Polity Press
in association with Blackwell Publishers Ltd.

2 4 6 8 10 9 7 5 3 1

Editorial office:
Polity Press
65 Bridge Street
Cambridge CB2 1UR, UK

Marketing and production:
Blackwell Publishers Ltd
108 Cowley Road
Oxford OX4 1JF, UK

Published in the USA by
Blackwell Publishers Inc.
Commerce Place
350 Main Street
Malden, MA 02148, USA

ISBN 0-7456-1433-7
ISBN 0-7456-1897-9 (pbk)

A CIP catalogue record for this book is available from the British Library and the Library of Congress.

Typeset in 11 on 13pt Adobe Caslon
by Photoprint, Torquay, Devon
Printed in Great Britain by Hartnolls Ltd, Bodmin, Cornwall

This book is printed on acid-free paper.

Contents

The self . . . is essentially a social structure, and it arises in social experience.

G.H. Mead, *Mind, Self and Society*

As a main focus of attention talk is unique . . . for talk creates for the participant a world and a reality that has other participants in it.

Erving Goffman, *Interaction Ritual*

Preface
and Acknowledgements

From 1974 to 1995, 19,341 social science books and articles have had "self" in their titles or abstracts or as key words (*Sociofile*, 1/74–4/95). The self is also a topic of major interest to philosophers, theologians, and literary theorists, as well as to the general public. Grocery store checkout lines display magazines entitled *Self*; "self-help" books are among the fastest growing sections in bookstores; and "self-esteem," "self-actualization," and "self-consciousness" are treated as major social problems. Oddly enough, the interactional creation of selves in talk has as yet been little studied.

This book is about how we present our selves in talk. It examines conversations as joint productions requiring trust, dependency, and coordination. If we recognize that the self is an interactional accomplishment, then we must also recognize that it is produced by multiple partners cooperating in the production of a social event.

Interestingly, perhaps the most fruitful avenue of inquiry into the nature of the self is only beginning to be traveled extensively. Talk is the principal way for others to know "who" we are. We are always aware that what we say tells as much about who we are as it does about the topic we are discussing. While language has been studied for thousands of years, the study of conversation (actual spoken talk) is a relatively new topic, with a history of barely 30 years. The theory and methods whereby to construct an understanding of this issue are at hand. The time to understand how selves are created and transformed in everyday talk is now.

The study of self-presentation in conversation raises a number of theoretical questions. The most general questions are these:

How are selves communicated?
How does that communication affect the nature of interaction?
How do those effects on the interaction feed back to alter the modes of self-presentation?

More specifically, I would like to know:

1 What is the role of talk in constructing a self-presentation out of the resources available to an individual?
2 How are identities presented, negotiated, and changed in talk?
3 How is talk used as a strategic interactive resource (one which can accomplish desired goals) to tell others how we see the situation, who we are at the moment, and how we see them?

This study is about how individuals tell each other who they are and how this affects conversation. It is about selves in conversation. In fine-grained analyses of a few conversations, it looks at

1 how talk structures interaction,
2 how gender differences are displayed in identity presentation,
3 how individuals manipulate support, and
4 how conflicts affect self-presentations.

This book is designed to appeal to students and professionals in sociology (especially in ethnomethodology, qualitative methods, theory, symbolic interaction, and conversation analysis), social psychology, sociolinguistics, linguistic pragmatics, rhetoric, speech and communication, and any other areas concerned with language use in everyday life. It should also appeal to an educated audience interested in how conversations reveal who we are and how we deal with each other in everyday situations.

Chapter 1 discusses Goffman's notion of the "interaction order" (1983b) as a separate domain of sociological study. It is in the interaction order that self-presentation takes place. Chapter 2 provides some philosophical foundations for the analytical portion of the book and attempts to show the connections between the symbolic interactionist and ethnomethodological approaches. Chapters 3–6 are analyses of conversation that attempt to show, as Labov and Fanshel say, "what gets done by what gets said" (1977, p. 71). Chapter 3 analyzes how pronouns are used to create interactional alignments. Chapter 4 enters the debate on gendered styles of talk. Chapter 5 examines how talkers line up support in conversation, and chapter 6 analyzes an instance of disagreement, its resolution and return to working consensus. The conclusions in chapter 7 return explicitly to the moral nature of interaction and attempt to provide an interactional account of how talk creates selves. An appendix provides information on the data employed here and the methods of collection and analysis.

The analytic portion of the book examines the fine details of how talk constitutes and is constituted by the interaction order and how in this order selves are created and maintained. It employs the insights of Erving Goffman, symbolic interactionism and conversation analysis to understand just what goes on when people come together. The goal is to provide an account of the self in interaction.

I owe thanks to a great many people whose ideas, criticism, encouragement, and support helped this project grow over many years. As a graduate student in anthropology at Southern Illinois University many years ago, I was first introduced to linguistics by Larry Grimes and Ed Cook. It was at a lecture by Dell Hymes at Southern Illinois University that I realized how fascinating and important the study of talk was. Though I did not meet him until many years later, it was his lecture that afternoon that changed the direction of my studies.

In 1979, I arrived in Bloomington, Indiana, to begin graduate training for a second time, this time in sociolinguistics. It was there that I met and began to study with Allen Grimshaw, Bill Corsaro, Donna Eder, Bonnie Kendall, and Charles Bird. Their influence on my work and on shaping my perspectives on language goes beyond my ability to offer adequate thanks. I continue to come up with ideas I think are new, only later to realize that they are indebted to those excellent and caring teachers. Allen, Bill, and Donna have continued to read drafts and offer encouragement, and I still depend on their wisdom.

I owe perhaps the largest single intellectual debt to Allen Grimshaw, who, for the last 16 years, has continued to bully, cajole, criticize, challenge, and encourage me every step of the way. He serves as my model when I think about being a mentor to students. The Multiple Analysis Project that Allen directed and saw through to publication (Grimshaw, 1989, 1994) provided the data for my dissertation (1985) and has also provided much of the data for this book.

I would also like to thank Anthony Giddens, who, as a visiting scholar at Indiana in 1981, provided the beginnings of my reading of hermeneutic and phenomenological philosophers and my appreciation of their connections to American pragmatism and symbolic interaction.

In the ten years since graduate school, the help of colleagues, students, editors, and the anonymous readers we all depend on to get us into print has been vital for the development of this work. Within my own small college, I owe many thanks to my former chair and close friend, Chris Smith, and to the members of Mount Saint Mary's Writing Center, Steve Newmann, Carmen Schmersahl, Sarah Sinopoli, and Byron Stay. I am especially grateful to a former member of the Writing Center, as well as a coauthor, Meg Tipper, with whom I collaborated on work discussed here.

In my ten years at Mount Saint Mary's, I have had too many students to thank individually. But for special help on this project, especially with bibliographic and interlibrary loan work and with copying and all the other mundane tasks of preparing a manuscript, I owe particular thanks to our departmental assistants, Alison Gibbons and Jennifer Tinder. I cannot imagine two more helpful, cheerful, resourceful, and imaginative researchers and feel truly blessed to have had their help.

I would also like to thank our departmental secretary, Rosilee Litz, and the staff of the Hugh Phillips Library, especially Lisa Davis, who handled that necessity of small college libraries, interlibrary loans.

Colleagues at a distance are also necessary for survival, and I am grateful for the help of a number of scholars over the years. Jack Spencer, Doug Maynard, and Dede Boden have provided ideas, critiques, and intellectual stimulation. For a long, informative phone call he may not even remember having, I am indebted to Richard Hilbert, who helped me put together a book proposal when I was struggling to get started. Finally I would like to thank Bob Sanders, who, as editor of *Research on Language and Social Interaction*, devoted an extraordinary amount of time and energy to helping move an essay from ungainly draft to polished article.

I must also thank Mount Saint Mary's College for providing many President's Pride Summer Research Grants and the support of a year-long sabbatical that have made this book possible. I am also grateful for the congenial working environment, our ongoing faculty book discussion groups, and the interdisciplinary delights of a small college.

I am especially grateful to John Thompson of Polity Press, who first accepted the proposal for this book and gave me the time and encouragement to finish it, and to Polity's anonymous reader who provided me with a very careful reading and critique of the manuscript and excellent suggestions for revision.

Finally, as always, I am more grateful than I can say to my wife Jane, my son Brady, and my daughter Megan for all of our talk and for their years of patience with what seemed like a never ending project that took me out at nights and kept me away on weekends. It's the talking we do in our families that teaches us what talk is really about and for. It's in that talk that selves are first formed.

Versions of some of the material in this book appeared in "Small disagreements: character contests and working consensus in informal talk," *Symbolic Interaction*, 17 (1994), pp. 107–27; and "How to do things with friends: altercasting and recipient design," *Research on Language and Social Interaction*, 28 (1995), pp. 147–70.

Transcription Conventions

[– overlapping talk and simultaneous turn beginnings
] – end of overlapping talk
( ) – unintelligible stretch of talk
(.) – each period indicates a pause of one tenth of a second
(3.0, etc.) – length of pause in seconds and tenths of seconds
CAPITALIZATION – stress, increased volume
:::: as in we::::ll – elongated utterance
= – no pause between utterances
? – rising inflection, not necessarily a question.

Lengthy blank spaces within turns occur when square brackets indicate alignments of overlapping talk.

{ } – author's inserted comments

_____ – underscoring is used to highlight a word being discussed, and does not indicate any characteristics of the talk.

1

The Interaction Order and the Self

If indeed "each person's life is lived as a series of conversations" (Tannen, 1990, p. 13), then it is in the flowing, reciprocal exchange of conversation that the self becomes real. Without such talk, the self would be inconceivable, because it would lack the symbolic medium necessary for self-presentation.

The self is immanently social: an interactional achievement, a "performed character," a "dramatic effect" (Goffman, 1959, pp. 252–3) that is the result of crafting our behavior so that it makes sense to others. Conversations and selves are both interactional accomplishments requiring trust, dependency, and coordination. They are produced by multiple partners cooperating in the production of social events. Talk is both the machinery and the product of such events. Selves live in the worlds that talk creates.

Talk is the principal way for others to know "who" we are. This book applies Erving Goffman's insights about the interaction order to our self-presentations in talk.

SELF-PRESENTATION AND TALK

Sociologists, anthropologists, psychologists, linguists, and philosophers all devote attention to the nature of the self, the social actor

1

who produces thought, emotions, rational and irrational actions, language, and society. What the self is and does, how it comes about, and its relation to other selves and the society around it are questions basic to all these disciplines. Like most important questions today, their study is not and cannot be confined to a single discipline. Understanding the self requires the integration of many lines of inquiry.

One of sociology's most serious omissions in its claim to be a "science of society" is the scant attention it has traditionally given to spoken interaction.[1] Linguistics has been a little better at recognizing the reciprocal problem – that the complex code it studies is in fact used by people in social situations to achieve real practical goals. However, most mainstream modern linguistics (with the exception of pragmatics) has more in common with mathematics and logic than with any study of how humans communicate.

One would expect that these two fields would tell us about how people communicate with each other in everyday life. But traditional approaches have resulted in a lack of interest in both the theoretical and practical aspects of the problem. Neither traditionally trained sociologists nor linguists are generally prepared to deal with the complexity of conversation, with its multiple meanings, taken-for-granted presuppositions, situational rootedness, and the many other minutiae of interaction which conversation researchers have described over the last 30 years.

One also searches in vain in the psychological literature on the self for a sophisticated treatment of conversation in self-presentation. Two recent works in which one would expect sympathetic treatment of these topics (Berkowitz, 1988; Gergen, 1991) are nearly devoid of interest in conversation. Carl Backman (in the Berkowitz volume) notes the absence of concern with conversation and its dismissal from studies of friendship and courtship, where one might assume that talk played a significant role (pp. 253–4). Talk and conversation are simply nontopics for Gergen's study of "identity in contemporary life" (1991).

Contemporary philosophy provides us with useful approaches to the problem, but its own biases toward written as opposed to spoken discourse create a peculiarly distorted picture of the nature of the self. Whether we turn to Ricoeur's hermeneutics (1981), Taylor's moral philosophy (1989), or Kerby's semiotic/narrative approach (1991), we find the same underlying assumption that the self is like a written text, worked over and composed like a narrative. Their preference is for language not talk. They ignore the rough-and-tumble of conversation for the more orderly confines of the text. Their work is stimulating and provoking but is not about spoken interaction, the place where selves are created, developed, and reshaped on a daily basis.

The study of conversation stands at an exciting threshold of discovering the connections between informal talk and the meaning of the worlds it creates. It is at this juncture that the reciprocal creation of society and self takes place. But crossing that threshold requires combining insights from a number of disciplines. We are ready to begin to understand how conversational talk constructs a social self. The work must be interdisciplinary. As Geertz has said, the most important, fruitful, and exciting work today is going on between disciplines, not within them (1983).

Theoretical bases

Four sets of related ideas provide the intellectual foundations for this study. Broadly, they come from ethnomethodology, conversation analysis, sociolinguistics, symbolic interactionism, and semiotics.

1 *Actions are designed for recipients* The first assumption, from ethnomethodology and conversation analysis, is that social actions are designed to "make sense," to be "accountable," to those who are their intended recipients. The meaning of actions is not transparent. Actions must be constructed and performed in such a way that a particular intention is conveyed, based on the actor's knowledge of "shared background expectancies" (Rawls, 1989a, p. 16).

2 *Talk is multi-functional* The second assumption, from sociolinguistics, as well as speech-act theory, is that talk is multi-functional. Because utterances refer not only to an external world, but also to the person who makes those utterances, talk is always self-referential (cf. Ricoeur, 1981).

3 *Self-presentation is semiotic* The third assumption, from semiotics and also from symbolic interaction and ethnomethodology, is that the self should be understood from a semiotic perspective as an "assemblage of signs" (Perinbanayagam, 1991, p. 12). Because talk is always self-referential and, as such, is metonymic, hearers interpret utterances as signs which stand for a larger self. Similarly Goffman recognizes that the "available repertoire" of "culturally standard displays" used in face-to-face interaction (whether gestures, postures, facial movements, or utterances) is composed of "sign vehicles fabricated from the depictive materials at hand" that actors use to create their presentations (1983b, p. 11).

4 *The self is the product of a moral order* The fourth assumption is basic to both Goffman and ethnomethodology and is also influenced by the work of Charles Taylor (1989). For Goffman, the sacred nature of the self, the respect for the self-presentations of others, the seriousness of presenting and protecting one's own face, and a commitment to the "involvement obligations" of interaction (1959, 1967) point to interaction as a moral order. For Garfinkel, social life is based on a belief that others are behaving toward us sensibly (accountably) and with goodwill. Social life works not because people follow normative rules, but rather because they follow constitutive rules which make sense of what is going on. Breaches of these rules do not result in chaos (or "anomie"), but rather in insult and anger (1963). For Taylor, "selfhood and morality turn out to be inextricably intertwined themes" (1989, p. 3). Identity is meaningless without connection, without an orientation in a "moral space" (ibid., p. 28) composed of questions about and attachments to valued goods.

These assumptions lead to a theoretical perspective in which it is understood that social actions are designed to make sense to those who participate in them. Self-presentation takes place in encounters, situations of co-presence in which "persons must sense that they are close enough to be perceived in whatever they are doing, including their experiencing of others, and close enough to be perceived in this sensing of being perceived" (Goffman, 1963a, p. 17). It is these face-to-face interactions that structure our behavior and our need to present our selves. Thus social actors are aware of the need to organize their actions so that they are recognizable tokens of the meanings they intend to convey or the actions they intend to pursue. They are "designed for the recipient," as Sacks said (1992, vol. 2, p. 230).

Mutual understanding results from a sensitivity to the necessity of *making sense* to others. Shared assumptions about sense-making lead to an exquisite sensitivity to the self-referential nature of talk. We are always aware that what we say tells as much about us as it does about the external world. For that reason, conversational talk always provides metaphorical information about the self. It offers others *signs* of who we are. Interactionist approaches to social analysis must be sensitive to this collaborative construction of face-to-face encounters, to the mutuality of conversation; to what Boden calls "the consequentiality of sequence" (1990, p. 254). For both Goffman and Garfinkel, it is this mutuality, this interdependence, that make interaction moral. This morality is not the result of external social organizational features, of norms, or values, or folkways. It is a morality intrinsic to interaction that is constitutive of interaction. Because interaction is meaningful, action is moral, and the self is of necessity a moral creature.

ERVING GOFFMAN AND THE INTERACTION ORDER

Over a period of nearly 30 years, from the early 1950s to the early 1980s, the work of Erving Goffman explicated the role of a third order in social life, neither institutional nor individual – what he named "the interaction order" (1983b).[2] From his earliest to his final writing, Goffman sought to describe how the interactional demands of situations are the primary source of structure for the social self. Interactional constraints are the product not of social structure, but rather of the needs of self-presentation. They are not the products of such standard sociological forces as race, gender, class, or age. Instead, they are cross-situational demands whose ends are "the creation and maintenance of self and meaning" (Anne Warfield Rawls, 1987, p. 143).

Rawls shows how the work of Erving Goffman, the ethnomethodologists, and conversation analysts converge on the description of "an interaction order *sui generis* which derives its order from constraints imposed by the needs of a presentational self rather than a social structure" (ibid., p. 136). Their work emphasizes the locally produced nature of the demands of the interaction order: that is, that interaction must satisfy self-presentational demands, while being "constrained by, but not ordered by, institutional frameworks" (Rawls, 1989b, p. 147).

In one of his earliest essays, "On face-work" (1967, but first published in 1955), Goffman establishes how the interaction order constitutes face-to-face behavior. He defines "face" as "the positive social value a person effectively claims for himself by the line others assume he has taken during a particular contact" (p. 5). Face is an interactive concept, dependent on the back-and-forth play of actor and audience. In this essay, Goffman describes the interaction order as a set of expectations so designed that "the person tends to conduct himself during an encounter so as to maintain both his own face and the face of other participants" (p. 11). Face-to-face interaction is then dependent on a "reciprocity of perspectives" (Schutz, 1970) between interactants, in which each respects the self-presentation of the other in expectation of being accorded the same respect.

This simple reciprocity profoundly structures our everyday dealings, by creating an order based on the demands of self-presentation, not social institutions. The threats which might upset this order, such as revelations of hidden, "stigmatized" information (Goffman, 1963b) or the loss of this respect in "total institutions" such as prisons and insane asylums (Goffman, 1961a), were insightfully scrutinized by Goffman for what they said about normal interactions.

In his introduction to the essays collected in *Interaction Ritual*, Goffman claims that "the proper study of interaction is not the individual and his psychology, but rather the syntactical relations among the acts of different persons mutually present to one another (1967, p. 2). The interaction order is "the behavioral order found in all peopled places, whether public, semi-public, or private, and whether under the auspices of an organized social occasion or the flatter constraints of merely a routinized social setting" (ibid.).

In an earlier description of the interaction order, he said that it provided regulation, "the kind that governs a person's handling of himself and others during, and by virtue of, his immediate physical presence among them" (1963a, p. 8).[3] It is like a set of traffic rules, which do not specify where people are going, only how they must treat each other while they are getting there.

Kendon points out that Goffman was at pains in the introductions to his early works to specify that the study of the interaction order was not to be confused with the study of small groups (1961b), the study of psychology (1967), or the study of communication (1969) (Kendon, 1988, pp. 15–17). The interaction order was to be seen as "a separate branch of sociology" (Kendon, 1988, p. 14), one which had not been adequately studied up until this time.

Perhaps the best account of the interaction order can be gleaned from Goffman's presidential address to the American Sociological Association (1983b), in which he lays out its characteristics, its basic substantive units, and its relations to and differences from the institutional order and social organization. Goffman lists ten characteristics of the interaction order, which can be seen as the essence of face-to-face interaction. First, interaction is relatively circumscribed in time and space (p. 3). Second, the interaction order results from "certain universal preconditions of social life," such as the need to share equipment, or space, or "access routes" "jointly, adjacently, or sequentially" (ibid.).

Third, is the "promissory or evidential character" (ibid.) of social life. This is what Mannheim (1971) and Garfinkel (1967) refer to as the documentarity of interaction. People treat face-to-face behavior as meaningful and read meanings into both our intended and unintended movements, and we know this and act accordingly. Thus behavior is semiotic; it is a sign vehicle for social meanings and is inevitably multi-functional and polysemic.

7

Fourth, face-to-face interaction involves a "joint focus of attention," and hence the "sustained intimate coordination of action" (Goffman, 1983b, p. 3) (see esp. Goffman, 1967). This observation is basic to both the symbolic interactionist concern with how people fit "their respective lines of action to one another" (Blumer, 1969, p. 84), and the conversation-analytic premise that talk is a locally produced sequential accomplishment (Sacks et al., 1974).

Fifth, face-to-face interaction means that people characterize each other both categorically, as members of "one or more social categories," and individually, in "a uniquely distinguishing identity" (Goffman, 1983b, p. 3). People respond to others in complex ways that may simultaneously reflect their uniqueness and their shared identities.

Sixth, interaction's spatial dimension means that there are territorial effects – what Goffman calls "personal territory contingencies" (ibid., p. 4) having to do with our vulnerability to both physical and psychic assault, as well as with our ability to inflict such damage. These contingencies mean that all interaction is entered into with an awareness of risks and potentialities in terms of treatment of and by others (see esp. Goffman, 1971, pp. 28–61).

This leads to a seventh characteristic, which is that potentially threatening behaviors are part of "a fundamental duality of use" of behaviors, such that vulnerabilities may be proffered as marks of courtesy or affection (Goffman, 1983b, p. 4). This essentially ethological observation is consistent with our knowledge of dominance and submission behaviors in many species. Human manifestations of deference are ritual resources based on the communicative potential of these behaviors (see esp. Goffman, 1967). This is part of the basis of my emphasis on the multifunctionality and polysemy of conversational talk.

Eighth, these territorial contingencies require a set of "techniques of social management" (Goffman, 1983b, p. 4), in which bodily displays are enacted and read as if part of a "natural theater." Once again, behavior is treated as meaningful and so must be managed in terms of its "recipient design" features (Sacks et al., 1974).

Goffman's last two points recognize that extra-situational factors must also be considered in interaction. Goffman introduces the notion of "standing behavior patterns" (1983b, p. 4) to remind us that people bring certain expectations with them to a situation. Finally, he also recognizes that individuals have unique biographies "of prior dealings with the other participants" and a "vast array of cultural assumptions" (ibid.) that they bring to any interactional setting. While Schegloff (1987b) wisely warns that we cannot presume the relevance of contextual features, such as race or gender, if there is not some conversational warrant for so doing, we can at least presume that people come to interaction with a store of experience and assumptions.

These characteristics of face-to-face interaction are a set of fundamental observations on the nature of our everyday dealings with each other. Taken together, they define an order of experience that is constitutive of social life. It is located in time and place, treated as meaningful but potentially (and of course, usefully) ambiguous and threatening, and semi-permeable to external influences. These characteristics are responsible for the orderliness of this order. Most significantly, they are products of social encounters, not of some larger social structural forces.

Goffman defines five "basic substantive units" that comprise the order. His units provide a set of concepts moving from smallest to largest, including actors and events. First are people, who are either "singles" or "withs" (Goffman, 1983b, p. 6) (see esp. Goffman, 1971, pp. 3–27). These are "self-contained units for the purposes of participation in the flow of pedestrian social life" (1983b, p. 6). Second is "contact," "any occasion when an individual comes into another's response presence" (ibid.). Third are the encounters "in which persons come together into a small physical circle as ratified participants in a consciously shared, clearly interdependent undertaking" (ibid., p. 7). These may be conversations, card games, service transactions, and so forth (see esp. Goffman, 1964).

Fourth is the "platform format, . . . in which an activity is set before an audience" (Goffman, 1983b, p. 7). The key feature of this encounter is that there is an audience whose job it is to observe, not to interact. Finally, Goffman calls the largest of interactive events "celebrative social occasions . . . the foregathering of individuals

9

admitted on a controlled basis, the whole occurring under the auspices of, and in honor of, some jointly appreciated circumstances" (ibid.). Such occasions, which may proceed over a number of days, may be, and probably are multi-focused, containing multiple circles of ratified participants and perhaps multiple platform activities.

This set of interactive units provides a parsimonious way of describing interaction. It defines a very small number of relevant units based on the who and what of interaction (people, contacts, encounters, platform activities, and celebrations) and shows how they combine into the stuff of social life. It is with or within these units that the ten previously noted characteristics of interaction occur.

Finally, Goffman makes clear how the interaction order is connected to the institutional order. The institutional order concerns the basic units of much traditional sociology: gender, age, race, and class. But the interactional order is not the basis from which these macro structures develop. Interactional units are not "prior, fundamental, or constitutive of the shape of macroscopic phenomena" (ibid., p. 9). They are rather the stuff of situations, of encounters, and while they are interpenetrated by the institutional demands of social life, they are part of "an interaction order *sui generis*" (Rawls, 1987, p. 136) reflecting self-presentational demands. This order is "constrained by, but not ordered by, institutional frameworks" (Rawls, 1989b, p. 147).

Goffman uses a variety of metaphors to describe the connection between the two orders. They are "geared or linked into" each other; there is a "loose coupling," "a set of transformation rules," or a "membrane selecting how various externally relevant social distinctions will be managed within the interaction" (1983b, p. 11). The claims of other prominent theorists (Giddens, 1988; Collins, 1989) not withstanding, Goffman is clear in his separation of the two orders. They are not just quantitatively (micro and macro) different. They are qualitatively different. They are about different problems.[4]

Wilson (1991) provides an ethnomethodological account of this same issue. He makes a distinction between "conventions," the "culturally variable, historically contingent and negotiable" categories of social structure, and "mechanisms," "the tools members of society use to construct their interaction" (p. 26). Whereas conventions are subject to change and negotiation, mechanisms are more basic. If they are changed, the very nature of the interaction changes. A change in the turn-taking procedure in mundane conversation – for example, from locally to externally controlled (as in a courtroom) – means that it is no longer conversation, it is something else, such as cross-examination.

This distinction draws on the basic phenomenological concept of essences (*eidos*). Wilson's mechanisms are the essence of interaction, its "most general, necessary, and invariant features" (Schmitt, 1967, p. 139), without which an interaction would not be that interaction. For example, everyday conversation is locally controlled. The turn-taking procedures of the talk specify that one person talks at a time, that turns are exchanged, and that the next speaker may be chosen by the current speaker or may self-select (Sacks et al., 1974). Any other speaker-selection system – for example, one in which one person controls the floor and single-handedly allocates turns – would not be constitutive of normal everyday conversation. The change in the basic mechanism of the interaction changes what we call that interaction.

By contrast, conventions change on a regular basis. The meaning of conventions such as race, age, or gender, are historically, socially, politically, and economically reconstructed continuously. They are resources to which actors may orient themselves: for example, beliefs about the nature of women or men, or old people, or politicians. These resources are employed in interaction, but they are not the machinery of interaction.

Goffman's concept of an interaction order provides a semiotic research agenda for investigating how behaviors indicate or signify social arrangements. The focus is on the connective tissue, rather than the organs of society. Here the interest is in how one order is linked to another, and there is a careful recognition that, while there are connections, each has its own ground rules and constraints.

Two readings of Goffman's interaction order

Kendon's reading of Goffman emphasizes that "the study of face-to-face interaction should be regarded as a separate branch of sociology" (Kendon, 1988, p. 14), a field, not coincidentally, to which Kendon's own work has contributed significantly (see esp. Kendon, 1990). As noted earlier, he shows how Goffman was at pains in each of his early books to distinguish the study of interaction from related areas of sociology like small groups, communication, or social psychology.

Kendon provides a brief discussion of Goffman's intellectual parentage and points to the influences of both Simmel and Mead on the kind of work Goffman undertook. He also distinguishes the sort of quantitative, measurement-oriented interactional observations made by researchers such as Robert Bales (1950) and George Homans (1950) from the more ethological, descriptive work of Goffman. Finally, he notes how influential visual anthropologists like Gregory Bateson and Ray Birdwhistell became in suggesting to Goffman how to look at interaction.

Kendon calls attention to the distinction that Goffman introduces early in *The Presentation of Self in Everyday Life* (1959) between giving and giving off expressions, between the intentional and the "symptomatic" (p. 2) in a speaker's words (e.g. between content and accent).[5] While Goffman points out that this distinction "has only an initial validity" (ibid.), since actors are capable of manipulating both informational tracks, it is important to Goffman's work for at least two reasons. First, it introduces the distinction between the specifically intended and the unintentionally meaningful information in a self-presentation. Second, it introduces a notion to which Goffman returned many years later (1974): how a message is framed by a variety of factors that provide its context. Hence meaning is inextricably tied to situational factors. The significance of framing to meaning will be discussed in the following section.

Both Rawls (1987, 1989b) and Kendon (1988) recognize that Goffman's conception of the interaction order makes meaning central to face-to-face interaction. Rawls puts a basic phenomeno-

12

logical issue, the "problem of achieving mutual understanding" (Rawls, 1989b, p. 148), at the center of her discussion of the interaction order, and in so doing shows how the work of Harvey Sacks and conversation analysis extends Goffman's own understanding. For Rawls, self and meaning are parallel accomplishments of the interaction order. Both are emergent, locally produced, sequential achievements of people in interaction. Rawls is critical of Goffman's inadequate and traditional linguistic theorizing and shows how conversation analysis provides a more appropriate conceptualization of what talk does. In this way she develops a more sophisticated account of the interaction order, one that treats self and meaning as intrinsically connected concepts.

Rawls (1987) provides a critical reading of Goffman's conception of the interaction order. She shows how Goffman's work creates a new way of understanding the relation between individual and social structure, an understanding that does not require choosing one or the other, micro or macro, as determinative of social life. She describes four elements of a theory of the interaction order.

First, "the social self needs to be continually achieved in and through interaction" (1987, p. 136). Thus self-presentation is a basic feature of the interaction order. This claim is theoretically important, because it shows how Goffman's work is tied to Mead (1934) and symbolic interactionism, a fact often minimized in discussions of Goffman's intellectual heritage.

Second, the demands of self-presentation in interaction "not only define the interaction order, but also may resist and defy social structure" (Rawls, 1987, p. 136). As noted earlier, Goffman's study of total institutions (1961a) shows how the interaction order resists the demands of social structure. Rawls describes this situation by claiming that "it is not up to capable agents to decide whether or not to resist institutional constraint. The interaction order resists these constraints in its own right" (1987, p. 141).

Third, "interaction is conceived of as a production order wherein a commitment to that order generates meaning" (ibid., pp. 136–7). Goffman (1967) calls conversation "a little social system with its own boundary-maintaining tendencies . . . a little patch of commitment and loyalty" (pp. 113–14). That commitment and loyalty are subject to all sorts of assaults which distract from the "conjoint

13

spontaneous involvement" (ibid., p. 117) necessary to maintain interaction. Interactants proceed with an awareness that interaction is fragile and that what goes on in the encounter is meaningful because it reflects a choice to maintain the interaction. Conversation analysts have developed this theme in great detail by showing the significance of sequence for the intelligibility of conversation.

Finally, this leads to a recognition of the basic moral nature of the interaction order, because "persons must commit themselves to the ground rules of interaction in order for selves to be maintained" (Rawls, 1987, p. 137). Morality, in this sense, does not reflect larger institutional values of the society. Rather, morality for Goffman is about a commitment to others and to the self-presentations they make.

Rawls's summary of a theory of the interaction order emphasizes self-presentation, the constraints the order places on social structure, involvement obligations, and morality. These features will come up again in the specific analyses of interaction presented in the text.

Frames and meaning in interaction

Conversational talk may be seen as an activity which frames the meaning of what is going on and makes it interpretable. The frames must be inferred from the talk, but the talk only makes sense when the appropriate frame is understood. Listeners must figure out just what the talker is up to. Since talkers are aware of this situation, they craft their talk with a sensitivity to how it might be interpreted or misinterpreted. We see here both the reflexivity and the documentarity of everyday interaction. It is reflexive in the ethnomethodological sense that interaction creates its own interpretive context. It is documentary in Mannheim's (1971, originally 1952) and later Garfinkel's (1967) sense that behavior is treated as standing for, representing, some larger meaning. Self-presentation and sense-making are then part of the same process.

In *Frame Analysis* (1974), Goffman provides a set of analytic concepts with which to examine how talk frames and is framed by other activity. Telling stories, rehearsing for a wedding, reading a

14

script, or exchanging insults are all frames within which the same words have different meanings, because "who" the speaker is in each case is a product of the situational frame, not some immutable identity. Saying "I do" during a wedding rehearsal or when reading a script does not have the legal implications it does at an actual wedding, even though the words, their intonation, and much of the setting are otherwise the same.

In *Frame Analysis*, and later in *Forms of Talk* (1981), Goffman develops this line of thought by decomposing the concepts of speaker and hearer into sets of constituent capacities, one or more of which may be operating simultaneously in an encounter. A speaker is an "animator," or producer, of talk, but he may or may not be the "principal" who is the source of the spoken words, the "strategist" who plans how the talk will proceed, or a "figure" in his own talk (such as a "character in an anecdote") (1974, pp. 516–39; 1981, pp. 144–53).

A hearer may be an "official participant" who is "addressed" or "unaddressed," an "overhearer," or an "eavesdropper" (1981, pp. 131–3). This analytic procedure allows Goffman to examine the "production format" (which capacities are producing the talk) and the "participation framework" (the relations between the producers and recipients of an utterance) of interactive situations.

In both *Frame Analysis* and *Forms of Talk*, the structure of conversation is shown to be considerably more complex than simply taking turns at talk and adjacency pairs. It is in this interactional complexity that identity work is accomplished. By identity work, I mean the activities that create the "situated identities" to be performed at any given moment (see esp. Alexander and Wiley, 1981; and Hewitt, 1988, pp. 112ff.). It is because we are more than just turn-takers in a talking game that more is said than what is uttered. Goffman examines the separation of the doer from what is done and in that separation finds the nature of the self. It is this theme that reminds us of Goffman's intellectual debt to Mead's analysis of symbols. Here we see an exposition of the symbolic relationships between what I do and who I am and how; in fact, it is the nature of the connectives (the talk) that is of particular interest.

15

Goffman's work provides guides to how that connection might be studied in talk. It provides a framework with which to examine how talk is used in interaction to create selves and hence how all social life is the product of such interchanges. His work demonstrates how the interests of symbolic interactionism and conversation analysis converge in the study of the self in interaction, and how it is the demands of interaction that create and maintain selves.

As Boden (1990) has said, the two disciplines share an interest in the "intertwining of meaning, shared symbols, joint action, and social order" (p. 265). Goffman's influence spreads to both disciplines, and his insights bridge the philosophical divisions of the two fields. His work illustrates how the self is a product of interaction, and thus a better understanding of interaction will yield a better understanding of self.

A further note on the moral nature of interaction

Finally I would like to briefly discuss Charles Taylor's recent contribution to an understanding of the moral nature of the self: *Sources of the Self* (1989). In this work, Taylor is critical of the modern procedural views that see morality simply as a guide to action. For Taylor, morality involves three axes, or dimensions: "our sense of respect for and obligations to others," "our understanding of what makes a full life," and "the range of notions concerned with dignity" (p. 15). The axes refer to others (obligation), value or meaningfulness (a full life), and self (dignity).

Goffman also recognizes that interaction takes place within a moral order, in that it requires recognition of obligations to others as well as concern for one's own dignity. His moral order shows the influence of both Durkheim and Mead, though it can be seen to go far beyond their conceptions. Goffman is sensitive to Durkheim's understanding that society is built upon moral sentiments that bind us together (Durkheim, 1912). Similarly, he is influenced by Mead's claims that the self is created in interaction and that identification with the generalized other is basic to a sense of self (Mead, 1934, pp. 144–64).

But Goffman's ideas about morality are most original in his discussion of the obligations we owe to the encounter and its participants that allow interaction to take place (1967). For example, Goffman's discussion of why queues are able to exist and why people wait in them shows how a moral commitment to the situation is basic to daily life (1983b). Rawls (1984) compares Goffman's treatment of waiting in lines to that of Sartre. She notes that from Goffman's perspective,

> the individual has an obligation, not because of his or her status within society at large as a grocer, for example, but an obligation occasioned by participation in interaction, to maintain a "working consensus" between participants, which makes certain demands on each other's performances. (p. 227)

For Sartre, waiting in line is particularly alienating because it reflects control of an individual by external demands. There is no intrinsic satisfaction. This behavior must simply be endured in order to get something else (Rawls, 1984, pp. 230–1). By contrast, for Goffman, waiting in line, or any other interaction, has intrinsic demands that are essentially moral, because they are obligations to the others present.

But Goffman's moral order ignores Taylor's third axis: commitment to or identification with "what is good, or valuable, or what ought to be done, or what I endorse or oppose" (Taylor, 1989, p. 27). For Goffman, the good is limited to the reciprocity of interaction. Goffman delineates only moral goods that allow situations to continue, that allow people to deal with each other. But his discussion of morality does not go beyond these choices.

It is Garfinkel's phenomenological account of the morality of social life that provides a connection with Taylor's third axis. For Garfinkel, "daily life is a morality" (1967, p. 50), because social agents must trust that another's actions make sense, are "accountable" tokens of some intended meaning. Garfinkel's various "experiments," detailed in his 1967 work, including some that breach trust (pp. 42–4), some that parody or simulate counseling sessions (pp. 79–94), and some in which students are asked to determine what people meant by what they said (pp. 38–42), show just how dependent interaction is on unstated assumptions about the nature

17

of what is going on. Heritage nicely summarizes Garfinkel's findings when he says that

> the "common understandings" achieved by the parties to conversations can only be achieved by the parties doing whatever is necessary at the time to "fill-in" a background of "seen but unnoticed" interpretation for whatever is said as it is said. (Heritage, 1984, p. 95)

Parties to conversation must presume a "reciprocity of perspectives" between themselves and the speaker; they must assume that actions are tokens, or "documents," of some intended meaning; they must take a "wait and see" attitude toward what the speaker intends, and assume that interactional meaning will be built up over time.[6] It is these assumptions that create the "possibility of mutual understanding," of a "shared world" (ibid.).

Garfinkel is not interested in the contents of those shared assumptions; from an ethnomethodological perspective, they are irrelevant. This model is simply based on the assumption that this mutuality must exist. But it is the assumption of mutuality that makes social life moral, and it is this presumption that leads to Taylor's third axis, which concerns "what kind of life is worth living" (1989, p. 14). Taylor contends that these judgments are inseparable from what it means to be a "self." For Taylor, "we are only selves insofar as we move in a certain space of questions, as we seek and find an orientation to the good" (1989, p. 34).

Taylor's third axis is what attaches the self to the institutional order. Taylor sees identity as a web of connections, not only to others but to "moral or spiritual commitment as well" (ibid., p. 27).

> To know who I am is a species of knowing where I stand. My identity is defined by my commitments and identifications which provide the frame or horizon within which I can determine from case to case what is good, or valuable, or what ought to be done, or what I endorse or oppose. In other words, it is the horizon within which I am capable of taking a stand. (ibid.)

Identity and orientation, then, are inextricably linked. They cannot be pulled apart, because identity is meaningless without connection, without an orientation in "moral space" (ibid., p. 28). For Taylor, identity crisis is not knowing where one stands.[7]

However, identity and orientation are consequent to the more basic moral relationship depicted by Goffman's interaction order. For Goffman, the interaction order is about reciprocity, and it places moral demands on us, which must be fulfilled in order for interaction to proceed. This sense of morality is constitutive of social life. Garfinkel's account of morality takes this one step further by showing how shared perspectives are presumed by interactants. Taylor's elaboration of three axes of morality cannot even be imagined without a foundation provided by these conceptions of an interaction order.

What is interesting about Taylor's claim is that just as the interaction order provides the constitutive mechanisms that make interaction possible, so Taylor specifies the next level of "transcendental conditions" (ibid., p. 32) of the self. The set of commitments and attachments that define the self are shown to be constitutive of what it means to be a self. Selves are not accidently attached to values and beliefs and others; they are constituted by those attachments. "One is a self only among other selves . . . . I define who I am by defining where I speak from . . . [A] self exists only within what I call 'webs of interlocution'" (ibid., pp. 35–6).

At the most basic level, selves are social entities. Mead recognized this in a way more sophisticated than James's simple statement that we have different selves for different situations. Mead (1934) knew that the self was immanently social, a conversation between our experience ("me") and our position at a particular moment ("I"). In this way, the self is emergent; it is created out of social life. Taylor also knows that the self is fundamentally social, "embedded in webs of interlocution" (1989, p. 36) within which the whole possibility of self-understanding arises from a language that exists only as a social phenomenon.

Calhoun (1991) points out that Taylor's discussion of self and morality calls attention to something often overlooked in sociological discussions of the self: the fundamentally moral nature of the self. Obviously, this criticism does not apply to Goffman and Garfinkel. The following chapters will describe just how the moral nature of interaction is played out in the events of everyday life. It

19

will slight Taylor's third axis, in favor of his first two, but it should be clear from the following analyses that the interaction order is a moral order.

Before proceeding to the analysis of actual conversation, I would like to provide briefly some philosophical and theoretical background for the approach employed here. This work draws heavily on both pragmatism and phenomenology as they have been developed in the sociological schools of symbolic interactionism and ethnomethodology and conversation analysis. Certainly, much of the preceding discussion of Goffman and Garfinkel relies on an understanding of that philosophical and theoretical material, and without some discussion of these foundations, material with which sociologists are often unfamiliar, many of these claims look arbitrary and ungrounded. By appreciating where the assumptions come from, I hope that the analyses presented in the later chapters will appear somewhat less arbitrary. Readers may skip chapter 2 if they are not interested in such matters and go straight to the analysis itself.

2
Pragmatic and Phenomenological Foundations of Interactionism

There are essentially two basic philosophical foundations for interactionism: pragmatism and phenomenology. Each has its own assumptions about people and social life, and these lead to slightly different though in many ways similar approaches to conceptualization and research.

The first derives from the work of the American pragmatists in the late nineteenth and early twentieth centuries, principally Charles S. Peirce (1839–1914) and William James (1842–1910), and later John Dewey (1859–1952). This line of thought was profoundly influential for the work of George H. Mead (1863–1931), W. I. Thomas (1863–1947), and Charles H. Cooley (1864–1929), which led to the variety of American sociology which has come to be called "symbolic interactionism."

The second derives from the work of the German philosopher Edmund Husserl (1859–1938), and its sociological elaboration by Alfred Schutz (1899–1959). This work led to the development of the schools of sociology called "ethnomethodology" and "conversation analysis."

21

Although these two philosophies developed with some mutual awareness and interesting parallels, they also have basic and interesting differences, which lead to different research agendas. For instance, while both reject a scientistic approach to the study of human social life (Adler and Adler, 1980; Schmitt, 1967), they follow very different paths to the discovery of their central concerns. For the pragmatists, symbols, values, beliefs, and an interest in just how social behavior works are the focus. By contrast, phenomenologists have searched for the essences which undergird the social world, "the universal structures of subjective orientation" (Luckmann, 1978, p. 9).

A very brief and certainly inadequate précis of each of these philosophical foundations will serve to introduce the conceptual foundations upon which the research itself stands.

PRAGMATISM

In the last quarter of the nineteenth century, the first truly American school of philosophy developed in the form of pragmatism. The logician Charles S. Peirce and the moral philosopher William James collaborated in the rejection of much traditional academic philosophy and the creation of a new method for solving intellectual problems. Pragmatism combined Peirce's interest in signs and sign relations as a basic theory of mind and communication with James's moral concerns about the practical consequences of holding particular beliefs.

Charles S. Peirce

Peirce is perhaps best known today for his influence on the development of semiotics, the "science of signs." He devised what he called "semiotic," as "the general science of representations" (1982, vol. 1, p. 174), as part of a project to put logic on a sound footing. For Peirce, signs are the basis of communication, and communication presupposes a community. From this perspective, communication is the product of individuals interacting through the use of a system of shared meanings instantiated in signs. Communication (and thought) takes place when there is a problem to be solved. Pragmatism for Peirce was a method to be used to study the meaning conveyed through signs (Thayer, 1967, p. 432).[1]

William James

For James, pragmatism was about social behavior more generally. He was especially interested in values, beliefs, habits (as learned behaviors), and the nature of the self (Thayer, 1967, pp. 433–4; Stryker, 1980, pp. 21–3). What is particularly relevant here is James's concern with the interactive nature of the person and all that implies. For James, instincts in humans provide only general impulses and are much less important than habits, which are socially (interactionally) engendered.

Habits, implying memory and intellectual life, account for the development of the various kinds of selves – material, spiritual, social, and the pure ego (James, 1981, originally 1892). The concept of the social self, which for James introduces the role of others into our image of who we are, comes to be of central importance in symbolic interactionism. This is perhaps James's most important contribution to an interactional theory of communication.

John Dewey

While Peirce and James are unquestionably the founders of pragmatism, it was John Dewey's synthesis of their work that made pragmatism widely available (Thayer, 1967; Meltzer et al., 1975; Adler and Adler, 1980). Thayer calls Dewey's pragmatism a Hegelian synthesis of Peirce's logic and James's humanism which attempted to overcome the modern problem of "the separation of science and values, knowledge and morals" (1967, p. 434).

Dewey's most important contribution to interactionism is the processual model of thought with which he supplants James's more static notions. For James, habit (implying a previous choice) is an evolutionary improvement over instinct; but it is still a static concept of essentially repetitive behavior (Adler and Adler, 1980, p. 26). Dewey makes two significant improvements on this concept. First, he sees habits not as repetitions of acts, but as "acquired predisposition[s] to ways or modes of response . . . a way of behaving . . . standing predilections or aversions rather than the bare recurrence of specific acts" (Dewey, 1922, quoted in Meltzer et al., 1975, p. 17). With this conceptualization, habit becomes a framework within which decisions are made. Those decisions reflect an interaction of past choices with present opportunities.

For Dewey, individuals and their habits exist in social contexts; hence habit itself is a product of social life. He argued that nothing is intrinsically a stimulus, but only becomes such under certain "conditions of action" (1896, p. 369). In other words, behaviors are generated by a response to what W. I. Thomas later called "the definition of the situation" (1937, p. 8).

This emphasis on the social situation as stimulus led Dewey to follow Mead in according centrality to the role of language, not only in human uniqueness, but as the source of a child's ability to mature and of an individual's connection to society.

George H. Mead

Mead studied philosophy at Harvard, where he met James. He was later a colleague of Dewey's at the University of Michigan and accompanied Dewey to the Department of Philosophy at the new University of Chicago in 1894 (Miller, 1973, pp. xviii, xxii). Mead's conceptions of the importance of language in social life resulted indirectly from the semiotic work of Peirce (apparently as filtered through Dewey)[2] and the idealism of the German psychologist Wilhelm Wundt (Miller, 1973, p. xvi). Mead used Wundt's idea of the gesture (a movement of one organism that calls forth an appropriate response from another organism (Mead, 1934, p. 14n.)) in much the same way as Peirce uses "index" – that is, as

24

a direct indication of the thing for which it stands (Peirce, 1958, vol. 8, p. 228). When a dog snarls or crouches or bares its teeth in a fight, that is a sign or a gesture that it is ready to attack. It does not mean that the dog is intentionally signaling what it has in mind, or that the other dog reads this gesture as if it signaled an intention. Rather, it is a direct sign of what is to come. Mead called the back-and-forth action and response of gestures that comprise a dog fight (or a boxing or fencing match) a "conversation of gestures" (1934, p. 43).

These behaviors are qualitatively different, however, from a gesture which has an idea behind it and which "arouses that idea in the other individual" (ibid.). Such a gesture is a "significant symbol." This sort of communication occurs only when a "self" is involved, only when there is a reflective process whereby meaning is intended and attributed. Thus Mead shows how human symbolic communication is different from animal communication.

Mead's discussion of significant symbols introduces both the social and the self into his account of communication. The Meadian self is a social process. Mead goes beyond James in developing a processual account of the self that uses conversation as its model. The self is a conversation between the "I" and the "me." The "me" is "the organized set of attitudes of others which one himself assumes" (1934, p. 175). The "me" then, is the past, the "habitualized ways of responding" (Miller, 1973, p. 170). Doubt arises when "the exercise of habit will not result in the completion of the act" (ibid., p. 91). The "I" uses those habits but is aware, because of the problematic nature of the moment, that they are inadequate.

The conversation between a habitual self (the "me") and an active problem-solving self (the "I") leads to new behavior, to a creative response to the world. Human beings react not only to external stimuli (as the behaviorists would have it), but to their own responses. This process, which is Mead's model of thinking, is possible only through the use of symbols which represent both the external and the internal world. People think by manipulating symbols. The self for Mead, then, is a symbolic process which results from an internal conversation. This is far more complex than the simple conversation of gestures carried on by other animals.[3]

PHENOMENOLOGY

At the beginning of this century, Edmund Husserl sought to establish "philosophy as rigorous science" (Husserl, 1965 (1911)), one whose goal was "to examine all phenomena carefully and take none of them as familiar or understood until they have been carefully explicated and described," a science that would be "descriptive" and "presuppositionless" (Schmitt, 1967, p. 138). "The goal of phenomenology is to *describe* the *universal* structures of *subjective* orientation in the world, not to explain the *general* features of the *objective* world (Luckmann, 1978, p. 9; emphasis original).

Schmitt (1967) defines phenomenology in terms of five characteristics. First, it is about "essences" (p. 139), or *eidos*. Phenomena are essences, an object's "most general, necessary, and invariant features" (ibid.), or, as Husserl says, "the necessarily enduring invariant in the variation" (1981b, p. 25). Phenomena are the features without which some object would not be that object. The linguistic method of distinctive feature analysis (Jakobson et al., 1952), in which the basic distinctions are those that separate two sounds (for instance, the presence or absence of exhalation (aspiration) which distinguishes "b" and "p"), is a practical application of the notion of essences.

Second, phenomena are intuitively discovered; that is, they are not empirical facts or abstract derivations. Since phenomenology aims at the development of a presuppositionless philosophy, phenomena cannot be derived from something else. They must be "derived from a scrutiny of particular cases" (Schmitt, 1967, p. 140). For Husserl, it is the process of experiencing an object that allows one to intuit or "grasp the object in the original" (Husserl, 1981a, p. 11). "Experiencing is consciousness that intuits something and values it to be actual" (ibid.).

This intuitive discovery process results from the third characteristic of phenomenology, what is often described as its method: phenomenological reduction through the use of bracketing, what Husserl calls a "phenomenological *epoche*" (1981b, pp. 29–30). In order to scrutinize particular cases, one must "bracket" or "suspend belief in the existence of objects" (Schmitt, 1967, p. 140). This is a specific method in which

> we describe an example and then transform the description by adding or deleting one of the predicates contained in the description. With each addition or deletion, we ask whether the amended description can still be said to describe an example of the same kind of object as that which the example originally described was said to exemplify. (Ibid., p. 141)

This method leads to the discovery of the "necessary and invariant features" of a phenomenon. It is this method that has led to phenomenology being called "more radically descriptive than any method of an empirical science could conceivably be" (Luckmann, 1978, p. 8). Phenomenology is radical in the sense of its interest in getting at the root, or base, of something. Using the phonological example given above, "b" and "p" can be completely described as bilabial (both lips) stops (a sound burst produced by complete closure of the mouth), distinguished only by the fact that "p" is aspirated (a slight burst of air follows the stop) while "b" is not. This description gets at the essence of these consonants. These claims are not empirical generalizations; nor are they logical deductions. They are defining characteristics of what those phenomena are. "They are true because they describe the phenomena correctly" (Schmitt, 1967, p. 138). If one of those characteristics were changed, another sound would result.

Fourth, phenomenological statements must be about intentional acts and they must provide the "criteria of coherence" (ibid., p. 146) of those acts. Intentionality is what distinguishes mental from physical phenomena. Consciousness is intentional, in the sense that it is about something. Thus phenomenology is about meaning and how people intend. Phenomena are intentional, in that they have meaning.

The final characteristic, coherence, is closely tied to the notion of intentionality. To discuss intentionality, it is necessary to understand whether an act is intelligible or coherent. "Purposive acts are not coherent and not intelligible (they 'make no sense'), for instance, where the action and the means used are inappropriate to the intentional object" (ibid.). Coherence may be the result of a particular sequence of actions[4] or of the appropriateness of actions, but in either case, intentionality introduces the notion of whether behavior "makes sense." This last concern is a primary consideration of the sociologies that have grown out of phenomenology, ethnomethodology and conversation analysis, and will be explored shortly.

Both phenomenology and pragmatism are attentive to the importance of signs for social life. Apparently independently of Peirce's work, Husserl wrote extensively about signs in his discussion of the nature of meaning. He distinguishes between indicative and expressive signs or, more accurately, indications and expressions – a distinction similar to Peirce's between indexes and symbols (Peirce, 1958, vol. 8, p. 228). Indications (*Anzeichen*), like smoke or fossils, simply point to something, but there is no meaning or intentionality involved. By contrast, expressions (*Ausdruck*) or expressive signs, such as language or facial gestures, are meaningful (Husserl, 1970; see also Schutz, 1967); they are signs of intentionality. This similarity with pragmatism will be discussed in detail below.

Alfred Schutz

Phenomenology as developed by Husserl was nowhere near as amenable to direct sociological application as was pragmatism. It took the work of Alfred Schutz to turn phenomenology into a usable foundation for social investigation. Schutz combines the influences of Husserl's philosophical method with the sociology of Max Weber and the thought of the American pragmatists, particularly, Mead, Cooley, and Thomas. Schutz saw the role of the social sciences as "the exploration of the general principles according to which man in daily life organizes his experiences, and especially those of the social world" (1970, p. 273).

Once again, I can only briefly summarize some of Schutz's relevant contributions for the study of interaction.[5] Three of Schutz's concepts are particularly important for interactionism.

28

They are the intertwined notions of the "life-world," the "reciprocity of perspectives," and "typifications."

The "life-world" (*Lebenswelt*) is "the world of daily life," "the intersubjective world which existed long before our birth, experienced and interpreted by others, our predecessors, as an organized world" (ibid., p. 72). It is "that province of reality which the wide-awake and normal adult simply takes for granted in the attitude of common sense" (Schutz and Luckmann, 1973, p. 3).

People deal with the life-world as "a world of well circumscribed objects with definite qualities, objects among which we move, which resist us and upon which we may act" (Schutz, 1970, p. 72). Schutz calls this perspective "the natural attitude," the attitude in which the world is "taken for granted and self-evidently real" (Schutz and Luckmann, 1973, p. 4). The natural attitude is neither analytic nor abstract. It is unconcerned with how perception operates or how the mind organizes knowledge. This attitude is governed by "a pragmatic motive," in which the world "is something that we have to modify by our actions or that modifies our actions" (Schutz, 1970, p. 73).

The natural attitude also assumes that the "world is from the outset not a private world of the single individual, but an intersubjective world, common to all of us" (ibid.). "I assume that the objects of the outer world are in the main the same for my fellowmen as they are for me" (Schutz and Luckmann 1973, p. 4). For this reason, there is a presumed "reciprocity of perspectives" (Schutz, 1970, p. 183) between myself and others. I assume that were I to stand where you are standing, I would see what you see; and similarly, that in order to understand each other at the moment, we are each able to momentarily give up (bracket) our biographical uniqueness and attend only to what is relevant to the situation, to the "potentially common objects" (ibid.). The relevance of this notion to Goffman and the interaction order has already been commented on in chapter 1.

This behavior is possible because the natural attitude is based on a named world, in which we relate to objects as examples of types; hence we assume those types are shared. Schutz says that "language as used in daily life . . . is primarily a language of named things and events" (ibid., p. 117).[6] This idea of the typicality of experience

29

presumes a continuum of experience from intimate to anonymous. The more anonymous another person is to us, or the less familiar a situation is, the more they are treated as types. The human "stock of knowledge" is composed of these "typifications," which reduce the infinite complexity of the world to cognitively manageable proportions (see also Schutz and Luckmann, 1973, pp. 7–8).

These three concepts provide a theoretical framework with which to understand communication interactively. From Schutz's perspective, people use a language that they take for granted and which provides them with shared meanings. They use linguistic signs with the presumption that an addressee will interpret the signs' meanings in much the same way that they intend them (see Schutz, 1970, pp. 200–17). They also presume that their interlocutor shares a "system of relevances" (Schutz, 1970, p. 204) so that intentions and motivations can be successfully inferred. This presumption clearly leads to problems when there is too great a difference between the perspectives or biographies of the interactants. With greater difference or anonymity, interactants will rely on "more or less standardized, yet more or less vague, conceptualization" (ibid.) or typification. This solution is only partially successful, as the frequency of inter-gender or inter-ethnic misunderstanding attests (see esp. on gender, Tannen, 1990, and on ethnic differences, Tannen, 1982, and Gumperz, 1982).[7]

Both these philosophies generate a world view in which symbolic communication is the central feature of human social life. Pragmatism's interest is focused on the development of the self and its social context. By contrast, Schutz's elaboration of phenomenology concentrates on the problem of mutual understanding. Not surprisingly, two related but distinct sociologies have emerged from these two philosophies. The next section will briefly examine these different theoretical orientations.

SYMBOLIC INTERACTIONISM

The philosophical work of the pragmatists led directly to the development of a branch of sociology which has come to be called "symbolic interactionism," a term coined by one of Mead's students to characterize the latter's work. Herbert Blumer humbly took credit for what he called this "somewhat barbaric neologism . . . that somehow caught on" (1969, p. 1). Following Mead, Blumer says:

> "symbolic interaction" refers, of course, to the peculiar and distinctive character of interaction as it takes place between human beings. The peculiarity consists in the fact that human beings interpret or "define" each other's actions instead of merely reacting to each other's actions. (Ibid., pp. 78–9)

Since humans respond to "the meaning which they attach to such actions . . . human interaction is mediated by the use of symbols, by interpretations, or by ascertaining the meaning of one another's actions" (ibid.).

Meltzer and colleagues (1975) cite meaning, social interaction, and interpretation as the three basic premises of all the varieties of symbolic interactionism.

> First, human beings act toward things on the basis of the meanings that the things have for them. Secondly, these meanings are a product of social interaction in human society. Thirdly, these meanings are modified and handled through an interpretive process that is used by each individual in dealing with the things he/she encounters. (p. 1).

Symbolic interactionism treats social behavior and thought as external and internal versions of the same sort of interactional process. Social behavior involves individuals making sense of each other's behavior by interpreting the meanings it signals, whereas thinking involves an interaction between the "I" and the "me" in which past (habitual) meanings and present contexts yield new meanings and new lines of action. This notion of thinking as sense-making is also found in ethnomethodology and is one of the key points of contact between the two theories.

Stryker's (1980) eight-point model of symbolic interactionism includes the three premises noted by Meltzer and colleagues, but explicitly adds social roles and "larger social structures" to the mix.[8] Stryker claims that (1) "behavior is dependent upon a named or

31

classified world" (see Schutz, above, on this same point), in which "shared behavioral expectations grow out of social interaction" (pp. 53–4). Among the named objects in this world are (2) social positions (statuses) and their associated behavioral expectations (roles), (3) other people as occupants of those positions, (4) oneself and internalized self-expectations, and (5) situations whose definitions constrain appropriate behavior.

Stryker utilizes Turner's (1962) concept of (6) role-making (1962) to point out that behavior is not just the product of naming, but has an emergent quality which develops through a "tentative, sometimes extremely subtle, probing interchange among actors [that] can reshape the form and content of the interaction" (Stryker, 1980, p. 55). The ability to make a role, rather than play a predefined role, is limited by (7) "larger social structures in which interactive situations are embedded" (ibid.). In this way, Stryker embeds interaction in an institutional context. Finally, (8) social change is the result of how much role-making is possible. "Open" structures which allow more role making will be subject to more rapid social change, as names, meanings, interactions, and structures themselves change. Stryker's structural symbolic interactionism is true to Mead's concerns about situating human behavior within a meaningful context in which the emergence of new meanings results from interaction.[9]

ETHNOMETHODOLOGY

The most direct and profound influence of phenomenology, and in particular the work of Alfred Schutz, on actual sociological research is seen in the parallel developments of ethnomethodology and conversation analysis. The term "ethnomethodology" refers to the study of "the body of common-sense knowledge and the range of procedures and considerations by means of which the ordinary members of society make sense of, find their way about in, and act on the circumstances in which they find themselves" (Heritage, 1984, p. 4).[10]

Harold Garfinkel

Harold Garfinkel's *Studies in Ethnomethodology* (1967) lays out a profoundly radical project in sociology. In it, he engages in the phenomenological project of creating a "presuppositionless" science by discovering the basis of social life in the universal principles according to which interaction takes place. Garfinkel takes Schutz's discussion of the life-world seriously by seeking to understand how "the most commonplace activities of daily life" are produced in a way that makes them recognizable or "account-able" to their intended targets (p. 1).

Garfinkel's re-specification of social investigation is radical yet surprisingly simple. He begins *Studies* by claiming that "the activities whereby members produce and manage settings of organized everyday affairs are identical with members' procedures for making those settings 'account-able'" (ibid.). "Account-ability" means that social actions are designed to "make sense" to others, to be recognizable tokens of intention. This simple claim leads to a set of ideas rarely encountered in other varieties of sociology. The basic notions underlying account-ability are documentary method, indexicality, and reflexivity. These are elaborated in a set of basic "accounting practices" (ibid., p. 3) which concern actors' use of knowledge and time.[11]

The first, the *"et cetera"* principle (ibid.), says that people both intend and hear that more is meant than just what is said. This recognizes that successful communication always depends on shared background knowledge, which includes shared culture, interactional history, and the basic Schutzian assumptions of "reciprocity of perspectives" and a shared "system of relevances" (Schutz, 1970).

The second, closely related "unstated understandings" principle means that "reporter and auditor . . . will have furnished whatever 'unstated understandings' are required" (Garfinkel, 1967, p. 3) to make the communication sensible. It refers to "what we both know is going on right now" (ibid.). This principle calls attention to a central ethnomethodological assumption: namely, that the meaning of any social action is unavoidably tied to the spatial and temporal conditions of its accomplishment (Garfinkel and Sacks, 1970). Hence what we understand to be taking place between us, whether it is a friendly chat or an angry dispute, will strongly condition the meaning of what we say and do. In this sense, specific activity is always in a reflexive relation with general understandings about what it means.

The third principle builds on the first two and refers to what Mannheim meant by "documentary or evidential meaning" (1971, p. 19). Mannheim says that in studying social action, "a datum which is apprehended as being there in its own right can, and indeed must, also be conceived as standing for something else" (ibid., p. 18). This is an action's "documentary or evidential meaning" (ibid., p. 19). In other words, we interpret other people's behavior as a token of some intended meaning. We make sense of what is going on by determining what someone is attempting to accomplish.

This principle builds on the first two, in that "what is going on" and hence what any action "means," its "documentary character," is dependent on both the "et cetera clause" and the "unstated understandings" of the moment. All three of these principles concern the very nature of knowledge in the "life-world." They attempt to specify how people know what they know in everyday social interaction. But these three principles are not sufficient to summarize that knowledge. The temporal aspect of interaction must also be invoked.

The fourth principle relies on Schutz's claim (which he credits to Husserl's notion of "polythetic" construction) that a sentence is built by the "step by step articulation of successive elements" (Schutz, 1970, p. 205). Garfinkel calls attention to the fact that interactions are "built up step by step" (Garfinkel, 1967, p. 3), and hence that many actions only make sense if we take a "wait and see" (Cicourel, 1974, p. 40) attitude toward them. "Over the time of their delivery accounts are apt to require that 'auditors' be willing to wait for what will have been said in order that the present significance of what has been said will have become clear" (Garfinkel, 1967, p. 3). Garfinkel refers to this problem as the property of "progressive realization" (ibid., p. 41). Cicourel calls this the "retrospective-prospective sense of occurrence" (1974, p. 87). This principle indicates that meaning in interaction is a complex accomplishment which is constantly revisable in light of future developments. Interactional time is recursive, not linear. Meanings are revised retrospectively and prospectively, as contexts are continually reshaped by new events.[12]

Finally, as a result of the previous principle, we must also recognize that the meaning of any action depends heavily on its "serial placement" (Garfinkel, 1967, p. 3) in an interaction. This phenomenological notion has been developed in great detail in conversation analysis and will be discussed further shortly. As conversation analysts have demonstrated, many items in informal talk attain their significance simply by virtue of their specific location in a conversation. For instance, greetings and leave-takings are recognizable not so much by content (their semantic meaning) as by their location. Greetings such as "How are you?" "What's new?" "How've you been?" can be said to "mean" simply by their placement at the beginning of an interaction. In fact, if treated literally, they tend to disrupt the expected course of conversation. They are "documents" which are read to mean "This is a greeting."

All five principles incorporate the features of indexicality, reflexivity, and documentarity such that "the most commonplace activities of everyday life" (Garfinkel, 1967, p. 1) are treated as unproblematic, transparent instances of meaningful conduct. These principles describe the taken-for-granted nature of everyday interaction. They are not cognitive rules by which individuals govern their conduct, as some have misinterpreted them (cf. the colloquy between Gallant and Kleinman, 1983, 1985, and Rawls, 1985). Rather, they are the "phenomena" upon which interaction is based. They are the "distinguishing and particular features" (Garfinkel, 1967, pp. 1–2) of social settings that make them what they are.[13]

HARVEY SACKS AND CONVERSATION ANALYSIS

Harvey Sacks (along with Emanuel Schegloff and, later, Gail Jefferson) developed conversation analysis as a field of study not as a rival to linguistics, or even as a better way of specifically studying face-to-face communication (although one might claim that these are both results), but because conversation provides "the raw material of specific, singular events of human conduct" (Heritage, 1984, p. 235). Sacks said that "sociology couldn't be an actual science unless it was able to handle the details of actual events" (1992, vol. 1, p. 621). Tape-recorded conversations provided Sacks with the sort of data that could be examined repeatedly and which were available to others for their critical scrutiny (ibid., p. 622). Sacks's project parallels Garfinkel's in its use of conversation as the data with which to examine how people go about their basic everyday behavior.

The conversation-analytic literature now extends over more than 30 years and runs to hundreds of sources.[14] I will review some central concepts in order to indicate the perspective of the field, though I must plead that what follows is an inadequate account of its richness and complexity.

The conversation-analytic perspective employs the basic ethno-methodological postulates discussed above. Conversational talk exhibits orderliness because it is produced in such a way that it will make sense to those for whom it is intended. Speakers and hearers assume that there is a reciprocity of perspectives (Schutz, 1970, p. 183); that the context of their talk, as well as of their interactional history, is relevant to interpreting the meaning of what is said; that sometimes they will have to wait to make sense of an utterance; and that the location of an utterance in an interaction is a key determinant of its meaning. Heritage claims that there are three basic conversation-analytic assumptions:

> (1) interaction is structurally organized; (2) contributions to interaction are contextually oriented; and (3) these two properties inhere in the details of interaction so that no order of detail can be dismissed *a priori* as disorderly, accidental or irrelevant. (1984, p. 241)

This approach treats interactants as intelligent, creative, purposeful social actors and presumes that the best way to understand social interaction is to take seriously the details of its accomplishment (see also the development of this notion by Giddens, 1984, chs 1 and 2).

Perhaps the most basic, and certainly the most cited, article in conversation analysis is "A simplest systematics for the organization of turn taking for conversation" (Sacks et al., 1974; hereafter referred to as SS). This formal model of the structure of turns and turn transitions in ordinary conversations illustrates many of the basic ideas in conversation analysis. SS starts with the presumption that conversation is the most basic form of talk, and that all others, such as chaired meetings, debates, trials, or ceremonies, can be described as transformations of the basic rule set (pp. 729–31).

SS treats conversations as economies in which the sought-after objects are turns. It attempts to systematically account for a set of "grossly apparent" facts about conversation, such as that "Speaker change recurs, or, at least, occurs. . . . Overwhelmingly, one party talks at a time. . . . Occurrences of more than one speaker at a time are common, but brief. . . . Transitions from one turn to a next with no gap and no overlap between them are common" (pp. 700–1) and so on. It accounts for these observations with a set of essentially syntactical procedures that allocate "turn constructional components" (p. 702) or units according to next-speaker selection techniques.

Turn constructional units may consist of single words, phrases, sentences, or groups of sentences. The important rule, however, is that turn transitions occur at predictable points called "transition relevance places" (p. 703). This system bases turn transition on "surface-structural features," and its value is that it predicts the observed outcomes.

Transition relevance places are located at the boundaries of turn constructional units. These places can be recognized in a variety of ways. Speakers may directly select a next speaker through a question, an offer, or some sort of specifically directed address. Alternatively, a next speaker may self-select by recognizing a sufficiently long silence or a syntactically or morphologically marked ending of a word, phrase, clause, sentence, or larger unit. Brief overlaps are predicted at these locations as either simultaneous starts or as places where a speaker fails to give up a turn.

Because of this allocation system, turns "have a three-part structure: one which addresses the relation of a turn to a prior one, one involved with what is occupying the turn, and one which addresses the relation of the turn to a succeeding one" (p. 722). Hence the structure of conversational talk is to a large extent accounted for by the need to connect it to preceding and proceeding talk.

This model is a system of interactional constraints "directed at achieving mutual commitment and reciprocity" (Rawls, 1989b, p. 161), which make understanding possible and structure conversation. It is distinctive in three ways. First, it is not psychologically (cognitively) based, in the sense that it does not purport to be a set of rules which interactants apply as needed. Second, it is not an institutional – that is, a social – structural model, at least in the sense that it is not based on collectivities for its source of orderliness. It is not social-structural in the sense of statuses or families or economic demands. Rather, it is a model of the interaction order whose demands have to do with meaning and self-presentation (cf. Goffman, 1983b; Rawls, 1987; and below).

Third, it is significant because of its ability to discover the structure of actual talk (interaction) in actual talk. Thus it is opposed to approaches such as generative grammar which prefer the invented examples of speech created by linguists' intuitions to the disorder of real conversation (Chomsky, 1957).

A general interactional principle characterizes this model of conversation. Following the basic ethnomethodological assumption of "account-ability," speakers structure conversational talk by orienting to their recipients (Sacks, 1992, vol. 2 , p. 438); by "recipient design" (SS, p. 727).[15] Recipient design is exemplified in three ways. First conversational talk is a "local management system" (SS, p. 725), in which turn allocation and turn size are local operations – that is, they are not pre-allocated. Second, these two basic features of conversation are controlled by the parties involved. Conversation is not only locally managed, but "party-administered" (SS, p. 726), in that the participants themselves decide turn size and order. Finally, it is an interactive system in which turn order is "contingent on, and oriented to, the contributions of other parties" (ibid.).

This design provides listeners with an "intrinsic motivation for listening" (SS, p. 727), because otherwise next turns could not be formulated. Likewise, understanding is to a large extent dependent upon sequential order, in that much talk will be a response to "first pair-parts" such as questions or greetings. Finally, understanding itself is displayed in the sorts of responses talkers provide. This is significant not only for intersubjectivity and local error correction (repair), but for the analysis such display makes possible.

Conversations are constructed on a turn-by-turn basis in which the architecture of the talk is the product of an orientation to being understood by the recipient of the talk. Intersubjectivity is thus not some internal problem about whose operation social analysts must endlessly speculate. Rather, it is visible in a publicly produced orderliness that results from the demands of interaction.

It is almost certainly not too broad a claim to make that all work in conversation analysis builds on the model developed here. The important conversation-analytic topics which have been analyzed over the years, such as openings and closings (Schegloff, 1968; Schegloff and Sacks, 1974), adjacency pairs (Schegloff and Sacks, 1974), preference formats (Pomerantz, 1984a), presequences (Schegloff, 1980), storytelling (Sacks 1972, 1974), topic organization (Sacks, 1992, vol. 1, pp. 752–63; Jefferson, 1978), repair (Jefferson, 1974; Schegloff et al., 1977), and even the organization of "nonvocal activities" (C. Goodwin, 1981), all refer in one way or another to this model (or to be precise, since some of these references pre-date SS, presuppose this model).[16]

Recipient design, while drawn from a phenomenological approach to language, nicely illustrates another point at which pragmatism and phenomenology coincide. The similarities between this concept and the various sources of self conception found in Adam Smith, Charles Cooley, and George Mead are striking.

A number of authors have commented on the influence of Scottish Enlightenment philosophers on the American pragmatists (see esp. Miller, 1973, p. xix, and Stryker, 1980, pp. 16–21). We can see a line of thought from Adam Smith's concept of sympathetic imagination, by which we are able to look at things as others do (1976, originally 1759), to Cooley's concept of the "looking glass self," "a somewhat definite imagination of how one's self . . . appears in a particular mind" (1922, p. 183), to Mead's concept of "taking the role of the other" (1934, p. 152). But Mead rejects what he calls Cooley's "subjectivistic and idealistic" psychology in favor of an "objectivistic and naturalistic" external and social approach (1934, p. 224, n. 26).

Mead goes beyond both Smith's and Cooley's conceptions by recognizing that the self is not just a product of the imagination, but rather a social product of experience. The mature self for Mead includes "the attitude of the generalized other," which is "the organized social attitudes of the given social group or community . . . to which he belongs" (1934, pp. 154–6). This basic feature of the self is, for Mead, interestingly enough, the product of the "conversation of gestures" of which interaction is composed. While Sacks and coauthors make no reference to Mead's idea, and admittedly provide a far more useful and specific conception of how intersubjectivity works, the concepts illustrate the parallel interests of these two philosophical traditions.

These philosophical and theoretical approaches, despite a great many differences, have a set of fundamentals in common. First, and perhaps most important, is the highly descriptive nature of their research. Eschewing abstract models, coding systems, and surveys, they prefer to study, as Boden says, "the world as it happens" (1990, p. 247).

Second, both focus on the problematic as the source of thought or reflection (see Hewitt, 1988, pp. 69–70). It is when habitual action is blocked or when someone's behavior is ambiguous that actors must deal with the problem of meaning in social action.

This is related to a third issue: namely, the centrality of sense-making and the meaningfulness of interaction. Both approaches are interested in how people "make sense," how they figure out what is going on, and so are able to get on with life. They are sociologies of meaning.

Finally, the importance of context, whether of "unstated understandings" (Garfinkel, 1967) or of definitions of the situation (Thomas, 1937): both recognize that meaning produces and is produced in specific circumstances. Context is both the constraint and enabler of meaning. While the demands of self-presentation and the rules of conversational turn-taking are trans-situational, they are always operating in specific interactional contexts. For this

40

same reason, conversation analysts can claim that their model is simultaneously context-free and context-sensitive (Sacks et al., 1974).

Symbolic interactionists have always recognized the importance of language, but have less frequently undertaken the actual analysis of talk. Conversation analysts have made significant progress in understanding the interactional accomplishment of talk, but have generally failed to address the nature of the talkers. Boden has recently suggested that symbolic interactionism and conversation analysis "come together at the intersection of language and meaning . . . where thought becomes action through talk" (1990, p. 265). Each benefits from the conceptual and methodological repertoire of the other.

3

Pronouns, Interactional Roles, and the Construction of a Conversation

Pronominal forms do not refer to "reality" or to "objective" positions in space or time but to the utterance, unique each time, that contains them.

Émile Benveniste, *Problems in General Linguistics*

Sociologists do not often write about pronouns. Despite G. H. Mead's famous distinction between the "I" and the "me" as aspects of the self (1934) and Norbert Elias's discussion of personal pronouns as the "elementary set of coordinates" (1978, p. 123) for an understanding of human interaction and society, pronouns are generally left to the linguists or the philosophers. The exception to this is the work of conversation analysts and sociolinguists, who look at what people do with language.

The general absence of sociological interest in pronouns is not surprising, though, since, as Benveniste points out, pronouns do not refer to any "objective positions in space or time," but only to a "reality of discourse" (1971, p. 218), a terrain which most sociologists have been more than happy to leave to other explorers. But it is precisely this reality that is the stuff of the interaction order and that must be investigated to begin to understand self-presentation.

The complexities of pronoun use should be of more than passing interest to sociology, because they perfectly illustrate the centrality of self-presentation to interaction. Conversations are populated with a cast of actors, present and absent, whose explicit character-izations and implicit known identities give shape and meaning to the talk. In a study of conversations among members of a food cooperative, T. Labov (1980) argued that collections or categories of people are often indexed in implicit ways by references to group membership, past activities or characterizations, times or places, or "plurals hidden in singulars." She calls these implicit but recover-able references "feature + people," suggesting that these kinds of references attach people to certain features (see also T. Labov, 1994). In the graduate student conversation examined below,[1] "those people" is used to refer to a "moral category" of people who share certain features. "Those guys" or "those people" is heavy with implication and must be read as an evaluation, not simply a reference.

Given the potential complexity of interactional reference, how do conversationalists know or think they know to whom reference is being made? It is within the context of the interactants' identities that the interactions develop.[2]

Speakers and hearers seem in most cases to know who is being spoken to or about and are able to get on with their conversations without frequent need for clarification. This knowledge is neither the result of some external institutional order which provides rules to follow (Wilson, 1991, p. 27), nor does it result from a cognitive model possessed by each talker. It is the interaction order with its concomitant demands of self-presentation and sense-making that provides a framework within which such practical knowledge is possible. With the help of Sacks's conversation-analytic suggestions about pronouns (1992) and Goffman's ideas about "footing" (1981) or interactional alignments, this chapter will examine how pronoun use is constrained by interaction order demands and how pronouns are used to create an interactional structure.

43

THE LIMITS OF A GRAMMATICAL APPROACH

The simplicity of the grammatical pronominal paradigms belies the complexity of their use. To say that, in talk, pronouns provide information about "who is speaking and who is listening" (Grimes, 1975, p. 71), and about whom or what they are speaking undervalues the richness of those categories. At first glance, pronouns seem to be ideal examples of grammatical paradigms in which a few distinctive features (person, number, and gender) provide a minimal set of information which structures the conversation so that co-participants can understand what is happening.

But it becomes clear when one examines real examples of conversation that "who we are speaking as" (Watson, 1987, p. 271) and "who" is listening are very complex notions. The creativity of pronoun use in everyday conversation indicates how people build particular types of footings or alignments not only between speakers and hearers, but also between a speaker and his or her own utterances. It is certainly true that pronouns indicate "who" is talking and "who" is listening, but those "who's" are very elastic. They are part of what Goffman refers to as the "participation framework" and "production format" (1981) or Levinson's "production" and "reception roles" (1988).

Two examples will illustrate this complexity before we go on to a more detailed examination of the problem. The first is an interesting piece of talk which Sacks borrows from Matthew Spier, in which "A kid comes into the parents' bedroom in the morning and says to his father, 'Can we have breakfast?' His father says, 'Leave Daddy alone, he wants to sleep'" (Sacks, 1992, vol. 1, p. 711). This is not an unusual example; we can all imagine such a circumstance. But it is certainly not explicable by reference to the standard grammatical paradigm. Why would someone refer to himself in the third person? According to grammarians, people shouldn't use language that way.

An interactional explanation of this sort of thing focuses on its reference to an identity or a status, and hence the rights and obligations that go with it. The speaker makes self-referential use of the third person and thereby claims a footing which brings into play aspects of the social structure: that is, the institutional role (father), which allows him to claim certain rights.

Further, we know that refusals are dispreferred responses to requests, and hence must normally be accompanied by accounts to justify the refusal (Heritage, 1984, pp. 265–73). If you are invited to a party, accepting requires nothing more than a "yes." A refusal, however, would almost certainly be accompanied by some explanation of why you cannot attend. Here, "Daddy's" refusal of his child's legitimate request not only involves a reference to his institutional (kinship) status and its implied rights, and an account of why the refusal is being made ("Daddy is tired"), but may also be seen as a distancing in which a third person, rather than "I," makes the refusal.

Finally, it is interesting to note the "creative indexical usage" going on here (Silverstein, 1976) in which reference to social status (Daddy) indexes the institutional order, while the need to proffer an excuse and use the third person (he) indexes the interactional order. Pronouns may be used to "shift" back and forth between different social orders.

In the second example, which comes from the graduate student conversation which I will discuss in more detail later (example 3.1, p. 59), "you" is used to mean "we," or perhaps "people like us." The question here is why not use the grammatically expected term? Here is the sentence:

In other words, it's like getting through this program ta get yur doctorate so you can go someplace an if you wanna teach you can teach. If you wanna continue to do yur own research you can. But then you're caught up in this tenure track thing becuz if you wanna keep that position you've gotta do other things and produce.

Here "you" is used eight times in 61 words, and in no case does it seem to be legitimately a reference to the addressee, to the second person singular or plural. Instead, because it refers to the speaker as well as her hearers, it seems to mean "all of us."

An interactional solution suggests that "you" avoids the ambiguity of whether "we" inclusive or "we" exclusive is intended (Sacks, 1992, vol. 1, p. 350). Grammatically, "we" is ambiguous; it always carries the possibility that the listener is not included in the reference. An interactional perspective recognizes that "you," perhaps because of its status as an indefinite plural or its use in phrases such as "you know," seems to function as a more personal substitute for "people" or "everyone." Its ambiguity lies in whether the speaker is included, and that may be inferred from the context. In terms of recipient design, it is sensitive to the hearer in assuring his or her inclusion. Hence in this utterance, "you" may be heard as an inclusive "we," as part of a claim about our shared experience.

Both examples illustrate that the complexity of pronoun use in talk has to do with the capacities in which people speak and listen. These capacities are what Goffman calls "footing," "the alignment we take up to ourselves and others present as expressed in the way we manage the production and reception of an utterance" (1981, p. 128). Footing is an interactional phenomenon in which we signal our momentary identity, our interactional role, not only through language, but often through gaze, gesture, or posture (see Levinson, 1988, p. 179). In the above cases, pronouns signal how to hear what is said by demonstrating the attitude of the speaker to the utterance.

Pronouns are a limited set of options onto which a much larger set of interactional categories is mapped. Interactional analysis needs to examine not only the structure that pronominal usages provide, but also the interpretive work that speakers and listeners must do to make sense of the usages, the shifts in footing.

INTERACTIONAL ROLES AND SHIFTING CAPACITIES

Some previous work

Norbert Elias's (1978) discussion of personal pronouns as models of a perspectival sociology is an exception to the claim that sociology ignores pronouns, but it is still a treatment that emphasizes structure over action, an interest in social positions rather than what people do with the words themselves. Elias does, however, make an important and basic point about the nature of pronouns. He recognizes that they are not roles in the way that sociologists typically use that term. Pronouns have a reference only within an interactional context. As Elias says,

> the set of positions to which the personal pronouns refer differs from what we usually have in mind when we speak of social positions as roles – sets of positions like father-mother-daughter-son. . . . These latter words must, within a given communication, refer always to the same person. Typically in one situation the same personal pronoun may be used to refer to various people. (1978, p. 124)

What Elias alludes to here is the indexical or situated nature of pronouns, and the difference between interactional and institutional roles. Pronouns label interactional roles, whose reference is tied to the demands of a situation which they index. But Elias does not pursue this insight to its interactional conclusions. His intent was to develop a sociology which recognizes "the multi-perspectival character of social interconnections" (ibid., p. 127), so that social analysis would be sensitive to the multiplicity of types of relations in which people are engaged. He was not especially interested in what goes on in face-to-face interaction, the site of pronoun use.

The linguist Emile Benveniste points to exactly why the sort of grammatical understanding of pronouns that Elias favored is sociologically inadequate. In his essay "The nature of pronouns" (1971), Benveniste shows that the grammatical model Elias relies on is language- or code-based, treating pronouns as referential signs, whereas, in fact, a pronoun is "the instrument of a conversion . . . of language into discourse" (Benveniste, 1971, p. 220). The reality to which pronouns refer is the reality of talk, of face-to-face interaction, of "parole," not "langue," to use Saussure's terms (1959). For this reason, Jakobson (1957) calls them "shifters," because with pronouns "the reference 'shifts' regularly, depending on the factors of the speech situation" (Silverstein, 1976, p. 24), as talkers and hearers take up different alignments to each other.

47

It is only when we turn to the sociolinguistic and conversation-analytic literature that a sociological sensitivity to these issues is apparent. Watson's (1987) critique of Elias does double duty by explaining to a sociological audience the inadequacies of a standard linguistic (grammatical) approach, as well as indicating the need for an interactional rather than a social structural approach. He recognizes the need for an approach that is sensitive to the multiple meanings and multiple capacities with which people speak. Thus he illustrates a far more important point about understanding the role of pronouns in everyday talk. Watson shows how pronouns are "part of society-members' jointly-held conventional apparatus for achieving orderly, intelligible communication" (1987, p. 264). A sociological understanding of pronouns must deal with the dynamics of the interaction order.

Pronouns are an important guide to "who" we are speaking as. Building on Sacks's observations about "we" and "they" as "organizational references" (see Sacks, 1992, vol. 2, p. 391, and below), Watson demonstrates that a grammatical paradigm based on the distinctive features of person and number tells us nothing about how these words are actually used. "We" and "they" may have singular or plural referents, depending on their organizational context. For instance, having called a crisis intervention center, someone might say, "I spoke with a member of the crisis intervention center but <u>they</u> couldn't help." Or an agent of the center might respond, "Sorry, <u>we</u> can't help you." Watson also points out that, in fact, it would sound odd to say "<u>I</u> can't help you" or "<u>He</u> said <u>he</u> couldn't help me" (1987, p. 270). These plural pronouns, then, are used by individuals to refer to themselves in their statuses as members or representatives of an organization. They are indexes of speaking in one's "organizational capacity" rather than one's "personal capacity." Watson demonstrates here how self-presentation – who I wish to be seen as at this moment – is the foundation of interaction.

Similarly, Grimshaw's (1994) example from a dissertation defense, "<u>We</u> have something for you to sign" (p. 351), illustrates an individual speaking in his organizational capacity as a member of a committee. Were he to have said, "I have something for you to sign," the singular reference would have been inappropriately self-referential in a context in which an institution, not an individual, was granting its recognition.

Grimshaw's detailed examination of how pronouns are used to mark "referential boundaries" is sensitive to interactive processes. Through an analysis of six cases, such as the one above, he examines how the boundaries of "collectivities" are "explicitly or implicitly signaled in conversational discourse" (1994, p. 312) and how talkers seem to deal unproblematically with the ever present ambiguities which pronouns tend to signal.

Grimshaw recognizes, as Watson does, that pronouns are polysemic, and that their actual use is far more complex than the grammatical models suggest. Grimshaw shows how "membership affiliation identification (MAI)" (ibid.) is signaled ambiguously by pronouns, yet talkers often (regularly?) have no problems with this ambiguity. My own data suggest the same conclusions, and I will shortly illustrate how the same pronoun can be multiply used in a single sentence to refer, apparently unambiguously, to different persons (see example 3.1 and the discussion of "we" below). Grimshaw's work illustrates once again the importance of understanding the machinery of interaction if one wants to get at how larger social groups manage to function or persist over time.

Interactional versus grammatical analysis

Goffman's concept of the "involvement obligations" of an encounter recognizes the basic issue that differentiates an interactional from a grammatical analysis of pronouns. He says:

> Here, then, is one of the fundamental aspects of social control in conversation: the individual must not only maintain proper involvement himself but also act so as to ensure that others will maintain theirs. . . . whatever social role the individual plays during a conversational encounter, he will in addition have to fill the role of interactant. (Goffman, 1967, p. 116)

Because pronouns tie interactants to the moment, their use is one of the basic ways that this role is fulfilled.

Sacks and colleagues (1974) make a related point when they claim that conversation is designed so that there is "an intrinsic motivation for listening" (p. 727). Conversational participants must be attuned to the flow of talk if they are willing or intending to be a next speaker. "The system translates a willingness or potential desire to speak into a corollary obligation to listen" (ibid., p. 728).

Rawls (1989) takes this obligation one step further, by recognizing that the more indexical the talk is – that is, the more it is tied to the situation – the more compelled a listener is to pay close attention. Sacks's first lecture (1992, vol. 1, pp. 6–9) distinguishes between "composites," which have a "prepackaged" or "portable" meaning, and "constructives," whose meaning is constructed from the sequential relevancies of the talk. "Constructives," then, are the sort of phrases that can only be interpreted by paying attention to the preceding talk. Rawls makes the point that, in fact, this sort of ambiguity, which is exactly what is introduced by pronouns, is the glue of interaction.

> The greater the degree to which the meaning of a word or phrase is framed in advance by a set of relevancies which it brings to the context, the more ambiguity and discretion will be involved in its use. The less meaning is framed by words in advance, the more interactants must depend on sequence relevancies to locate meaning and the less ambiguity and discretion there will actually be. (Rawls, 1989b, p. 164)

The use of pronouns in conversation requires participants to pay close attention, to honor their "involvement obligations," in order to understand what is taking place. As indexicals, pronouns have meanings only in terms of their situational relevancies. When Benveniste says that pronouns refer only to the utterance that produced them, he makes the same point. Instead of avoiding ambiguity, conversationalists thrive on it, to maintain active co-participation.

Sacks's observations provide a foundation upon which to build a sociological analysis of pronouns. When they are combined with Goffman's discussion of "footing," it is possible to begin to understand how conversation depends on a referential structure created on the spot which is flexible enough to adapt to multiple inter-actants and multiple references and which creates both mutual understanding and maximum involvement (see also Tannen, 1985).

Sacks's interactional treatment of pronouns

Perhaps the earliest interactionally sensitive work on pronouns comes from Harvey Sacks's lectures. Here Sacks begins to work out (a project unfortunately never completed) what speakers are "really" doing when they use pronouns. His various lectures on this topic between 1965 and 1971[3] introduce a number of issues not pre-viously explored in pronoun use. These include why "you" often replaces "we" (1992, vol. 1, pp. 568–77), to whom "we" might refer (ibid., pp. 333–40), the choice of different pronouns as indicators of institutional affiliation (1992, vol. 2, pp. 391–5), possessive ver-sus affiliative uses of pronouns (1992, vol. 1, pp. 382–8, 605–9), and referential ambiguity in the use of "they" (1992, vol. 2, pp. 182, 291, 391–5).

A few basic conclusions can be drawn from these lectures. First, Sacks treats pronouns as part of a category of "pro-terms" that serve not merely to refer back to nouns or verbs, but rather to tie utterances together. The transformation of a stretch of preceding talk which is accomplished by the use of a pronoun is an immediate demonstration of understanding of that talk. "What such an utterance as 'They did' shows is that 'John and Lisa' are seen as a plural unit, such that this third person pronoun, 'they,' is the product of an operation on 'John and Lisa'" (1992, vol. 1, p. 719). By tying one's utterance to a previous one, a speaker displays an understanding of what has gone before, and so displays involve-ment.

For instance, when someone says, "That's just what I mean," not only does "I" index the interactive location of the utterance (who is doing the meaning), but "That's" ties this utterance to a previous one and shows how this piece of talk is relevant to what has gone before (ibid., pp. 150–6), and in so doing, shows understanding (ibid., p. 733). Or "I still say" (ibid., pp. 736–7) can be seen to reference not only an earlier utterance that "I" made, but also the fact that someone else has disagreed with it. So the phrase marks the presence of an argument as well as tying at least two previous turns to the present one. This notion of "tying techniques" can be seen as an operationalization of Goffman's ideas about involvement obligations. Pronoun use can be studied as a concrete example of just how interactants signal their involvement.

In a similar fashion, Tannen (1985) discusses how oral versus written discourse is characterized by a whole set of "conversational strategies," such as "cooperative overlap," "exaggerated para-linguistic features," and "frequent storytelling," which all signal "relative focus on interpersonal involvement" instead of on content or information. Tannen and Sacks approach the problem in slightly different ways, but both recognize that the presence of communication about the interaction, or communication that signals that understanding has occurred is necessary for the encounter to continue.

Second, involvement is also displayed by a sensitivity to the hearer's interactional role or footing and this is demonstrated by the recipient design features of pronoun selection (Sacks, 1992, vol. 2, pp. 444–6). For instance, choices of possessives such as "my" or "our" reflect addressee identity in uses such as "my" versus "our" mother. Again, this is not simply a question of politeness. These choices signal the talker's understanding of what is going on, and of his or her relation to an addressee or audience or both. Incorrect choice of pronouns means that the utterance has not been properly designed with regard to its recipient, and hence the entire sequence fails.

Finally, pronouns create or index categorical and organizational references, and in so doing can tie an interaction to a larger social structure. Hearers have a dual task of disambiguation, requiring them to pay attention to the talk and consider the nature of the implied connections. Pronouns imply categorical memberships. But because they have meaning only in terms of "situational rele-vancies," hearers must interpret, or as Sacks says, engage in "some sort of analysis" (1992, vol. 1, p. 719) in order to decipher the reference. For instance, "you in English is . . . systematically ambiguous, in that it does not discriminate between singular and plural usage" (ibid., p. 165). Hence hearers, in the process of figuring out to whom the "you" refers, must also consider whether the word is tying them to some others in some categorical fashion.

In an example to be considered in more detail shortly, David (from the graduate student conversation) says, "How kin you maintain yur integrity?" It is clear from the context that the "you" used here is not directed at any one hearer, but is rather a general question directed at his audience. But his audience must figure out that it is a generally addressed question, and then consider the category (in this case, people soon to be employed) in which this question places them. Sacks calls attention to the indexical work done by pronouns by showing how they function as conversational integrators as well as categorical markers.

Similarly, Sacks shows how "he" can also be a categorical referent in such interesting examples as the father saying to his small son, "Leave Daddy alone, he wants to sleep" (ibid., p. 711), or a report of a phone call between President Johnson and former President Truman in which Truman, who is speaking to the President, says: "I think I ought to report to the President. He might want me to do something" (ibid.). In the first case, the third person singular reference is self-referential (he – Daddy) and in the second, it is directed at the addressee. Both usages appear to violate grammatical rules, but interactants apparently find them perfectly clear. What they do is index the social status of one of the interactants, thus marking its relevance to the talk.

Sacks also shows how the "systematic alternation" of "we" and "they" reflects not simply plurality but their use to denote organizational membership (ibid., p. 713), as in the examples from Watson above.

Sacks's analysis of pronouns is spread out over a number of lectures covering six years. He contributed to the project in a piecemeal fashion and never systematized it in a single place. However we can pull together what he had to say and see a three-pronged approach that emphasizes involvement obligations, recipient design, and category membership. These three features of pronoun use are intertwined, each of them involving the other two.

The tying techniques that signal understanding must be constrained by recipient design and reference to some specific categories. Sacks provides a way of looking at pronouns that is sociological rather than grammatical. It is sociological in the sense that it focuses on the social location of the speakers and hearers and on what gets done by the talk.

Goffman on interactional roles

Goffman believed that

the language that students have drawn on for talking about speaking and hearing is not well adapted to its purpose. . . . It is too gross to provide us with much of a beginning. It takes global folk categories (like speaker and hearer) for granted instead of decomposing them into smaller, analytically coherent elements. (1981, p. 129)

His approach to this problem is to decompose the categories of speaker and hearer into their constituent elements based on situational as opposed to individual characteristics. This approach is faithful to his claim in the preface to *Interaction Ritual* that "the proper study of interaction is not the individual and his psychology, but rather the syntactical relations among the acts of different persons mutually present to one another" (Goffman, 1967, p. 2). Here speech production and interactional participation are the formats within which the "syntactical relations" of a situation of talk occur. These relations are the shifting interactional alignments referred to as the changing "footings" we adopt as a conversation proceeds. "A change in footing implies a change in the alignment we take up to ourselves and the others present as expressed in the way we manage the production or reception of an utterance" (Goffman, 1981, p. 128).[4]

For Goffman, "speaker" is a multiplex category better understood as a "production format" composed of five capacities, all or some of which may be called into play in any utterance. The capacities include (1) the animator or emitter of an utterance, (2) the author or composer of the string of words uttered, (3) the principal or person whose position is represented by those words, (4) the strategist, who decides how to proceed, and (5) the figures or characters who are performed by the speaker (on these last two capacities, see Goffman, 1974, pp. 523–37).

While these capacities may be congruent, it is just as easy to imagine their separation. Television coverage of former President Reagan's attempted answers to the press being drowned out by his subordinates' "No comment" nicely illustrates these separations. Hearers would not be surprised to learn that while President Reagan was the animator of his utterances, he was neither the ultimate source of the positions (principal), nor their composer (author), nor even the one who chose how to proceed at a particular moment (strategist).

Goffman replaces hearer with "participation framework," and in so doing changes the focus of analysis from the social status of the hearer to the context in which an utterance is made. A participation framework is "the circle, ratified and unratified, in which the utterance is variously received, and in which individuals have various participation statuses, one of which is animator" (1981, p. 226). One's participation status then is the position(s) one occupies in the framework.

The concept of participation framework points out the distinction between the act of hearing and the social slot of hearer. Hearing can result from being a "ratified" or official participant in a talk or an unofficial hearer (unintentional overhearer or intentional eavesdropper). The social slot of hearer, or recipient, may be an addressed recipient or (in a conversation of three or more persons) an unaddressed recipient (ibid., pp. 131–3).[5]

Speakers can speak in a number of different capacities simultaneously or serially and can treat their hearers as different sorts of objects as well. Speakers may utter words of their own choosing (author), representing their own views (principal), to gain a particular end (strategist), appearing to be no one other than themselves (natural figure). But just as easily, they can speak words uttered or written by someone else, play "devil's advocate," speak as if they were another person, or even an animal or supernatural being.

Some speakers, in fact, may treat all their hearers as audience and provide them with a verbal performance which seeks only appreciation, not actual participation. Rounds of storytelling in casual conversation come to resemble such a situation, in which participants take turns as narrator and audience, rather than as conversational interactants. In that case, hearers await their turn to give their own performance and, while expressing appreciation for a previous performance, do not treat it as a contribution upon which they are building. The difference is one between serial events and interactive events. One last point ought to be made here about the significance of this set of underlying features. By appreciating the complex array of elements involved in a conversational situation, it is possible to understand what is being accomplished by talkers and hearers. These multiple capacities allow talkers to construct utterances which are at multiple removes from themselves ("He said that she said that Frank saw me doing . . .") and thus tell stories whose restrictions are cognitive only, rather than syntactic. In other words, speakers are able, within the bounds of memory and attention, to tell stories, even about themselves, that are sufficiently distant from the present situation to be less likely to risk violating rules of modesty, censorship, or in general "the accommodative pattern of face-to-face interaction" (Goffman, 1974, p. 546).

An example from the graduate student conversation illustrates this nicely:

Rich: Well what, but what I'm saying to you is that I bet on those exams. I had to change self image by way of those exams and I just, compared to people that even, like H, those kinds of people, I think I put in more hours.

Rich is not just talking about the exams. He is telling a story about someone, who happens to be himself two years ago. He is treading close to the edge of immodesty, but is able to tell us that "I" in his story studied harder than someone else (and "those kinds of people"), someone his listeners all know is one of the top students.

The embedding at the beginning, "what I'm saying to you is," brackets the story, in the sense that it tells the listener that what follows is a formulation of what has just been said. The embedded nature of the story produces what Goffman calls a "lamination" (1974, p. 82), which in its innermost layer discusses studying for an exam. But in other layers, Rich tells (1) why he studied as he did (to change self-image), (2) how the quantity of his work compared to someone else's (it was greater), and (3) in some sort of overall layer, the kind of person he was and by implication, without undue modesty, is. Embeddings and laminations are transformations which connect capacities and kinds of figures in constantly shifting structures so that complexly layered characters are produced.

Levinson (1988) also argues that traditional linguistic, as well as communication theory, approaches are inadequate to a full understanding of what is going on in talk. Neither approach is able to deal adequately with how "utterances are semantically or pragmatically anchored to their situation of utterance" (Levinson, 1988, p. 163). For instance, neither linguistics nor speech-act theory distinguishes between "hearer" and "addressee" (ibid., p. 164). He believes that Goffman's concept of "footing" offers a solution to this problem, because it focuses on the crucial issue of "participant role" (ibid., p. 163).

Levinson adopts Goffman's approach of decomposing "speaker" and "hearer" into their constituent concepts. But he argues that Goffman's categories are still not sufficient, largely because Goffman does not distinguish between the larger context of a "speech event" (e.g. a conversation) and a particular utterance, which he calls an "utterance event" (e.g. a single turn at talk) (ibid., p. 167). For instance, Goffman's categories do not directly address problems such as multiple animators in a situation of simultaneous translation, or the distinction between source and transmitter in direct versus indirect quotation, or the problem of participation in a speech event (e.g. a nonlistening audience member) versus attentiveness to an utterance (an act necessary for the utterance event to succeed) (ibid., pp. 176–8).

Levinson's solution to this problem is to attempt to systematize Goffman's "production format" and "participation framework," which he changes to "production roles" and "reception roles." He decomposes each of these into a set of four underlying features, or dimensions, which then yield the specific "participant roles." The result, which he calls "a first approximation," and which need not be discussed in detail here, yields a more consistent, if still not fully satisfactory, breakdown of all the capacities involved in speaking and hearing in an interaction.[6]

In terms of pronouns, all this terminological decomposition is useful in illustrating the complexity and transitory nature of interactional roles underlying talk. The indexicality of talk, its unalterable connectedness to a particular situation, is played out in pronoun choices which create alignments between talkers and their topics and their hearers that must be attended to in order that conversation continue. Footings shift continuously in a seamless display of close attention to the sequential production of meaning, and in so doing demonstrate that interactants are attuned to the moment, to fulfilling their involvement obligations.

Both Goffman's and Levinson's elaboration of interactional capacities suggest the structural complexity of conversation. They show that talkers and hearers have a number of possible overlapping functions and that an utterance does not have just recipients and nonrecipients, but "an array of structurally differentiated possibilities, establishing the participation framework in which the speaker will be guiding his delivery" (Goffman, 1981, p. 137).

In this way we arrive at a set of elements that should provide the analytical equipment to understand what is going on in informal talk. What becomes clear from an interactional consideration of the role of pronouns in talk is how central self-presentation is to any satisfactory account of talk; a consideration left out by grammatical explanations.

SPECIFICS OF PRONOUN USE

Sacks's presentation of the inherent ambiguity of pronoun use and Goffman's account of the changing capacities that interactants can move in and out of both suggest the complexity of conversational interaction. It is through the use of personal reference, especially pronominal reference, that speakers tell hearers what capacities have been invoked.

Shifting reference

The following discussion will examine how the various pronouns of American English have multiple meanings that are disambiguated by their sequential context and how their references are part of the shifting alignments of conversation.

I have included the following rather lengthy transcript of a single episode from the graduate student conversation because it contains such a wide range of pronominal uses. This episode has a definite beginning and end that set it off from what precedes it and what follows. It is set off topically by its focus on the problem of the relation between authority and integrity. It begins with a question about what can be done about a particular problem and ends with an example of the problem's resolution. The nature of the resolution leads to a new turn but now with a changed focus.

Example 3.1*

```
 1  Amy:     I'm not sure I want those people
 2           [(that you mention)
 3  David:   [HOW kin you mainTAIN yur integrity?
 4  Amy:     involved in any social any kind of social
 5           change.
 6  David:   How kin you maintain   [yur integrity
 7  Amy:                            [I'm not sure I want
 8           [the whole field of sociology pushed into
 9  Rich:    [(Wait) No no if those if those people were
10           involved in in social change they wouldn't be
11           those those people Don't YOU SEE that?
12  Amy:     I KNO:::W
13  Rich:    (           ) I keep saying knowledge
14           is a personal statement. It changes
15           (your/their?) [goddam heads around
16  David:                 [(Right) How do you maintain
```

59

```
17              your integrity? Once you get the legitimate
18              authority behind you, you begin to loose your
19              integrity to a certain extent.
20              (1.5)
21   Amy:       If you   [take it on
22   Kathy:              [(I don't know whether)   you must
23   Amy:       If you take it on
24              (2.0)
25   Rich:      Now it depends on whether you're on the
26              [tenured                        tenure track
27   Kathy:     [If ya take it seriously
28   Rich:      And see thats like the conclusion I've had to
29              come with   [in my life
30   Amy:                   [Yeah
31   Rich:      is you CAN'T be on the tenure track ya gotta
32              give up the fact that they're not gonna think
33              yur Herbert {sic} Blalock if yur [gonna make
34              some statements that goddam
35   Amy:                                         [Yeah
36   Rich:      matter =
37   David:     = Right
38   Rich:      Because to be Herbert {sic} Blalock
39              [is              ta give up the stateme =
40   David:     [Right     Exactly
41   Amy:       = The problem is ta is ta learn to do without
42              their rewards
43   David:     Right exac of  [  i    ok
44   Pat:                      [But then ya can't keep doin
45              what y wanna do. I mean   [(ya          )
46   David:                               [And that's the
47              crisis that Rich has been facing. You can't,
48              if ya, if you want the rewards you can't
49              continue ta do what you wa wanna do
50   Amy:       Wha d'ya mean?
51   David:     If you want to =
52   Amy:       = [(            )
53   Pat:       = [In other words, it's like getting through
54              this program ta get yur doctorate so you can go
```

55		someplace an if you wanna teach you can teach.
56		If you wanna continue ta do yur own research
57		you can. But then you're caught up in this
58		tenure track thing becuz if you wanna keep that
59		position you've gotta do [other things and
60		produce
61	Amy:	[Sure
62	. David:	[Right
63	Pat?:	Right
64	Amy:	There's always [a new
65	Pat:	[You can't
66	Amy:	There has to be a point where you say
67		[( )
68	Rich:	[Yeah An I'm saying I'm saying the point is
69		the pi tha, you should, that we should teach
70		graduate students, we should teach graduate
71		students, US, WHAT our responsibility is ta
72		young graduate students is ta make sure those
73		goddamn people know it before they get down ta
74		Tom Maxwell's place and through all of that
75		pain [we've gotta shut (it off) early
76	David:	[Well we I We've done it effec Somebody's
77		done it pretty effectively this year if all
78		the students have left.
79	Amy:	Yeah
80	?:	laughter

* See Transcription Conventions, page xiv.

The basic pronominal structure of this episode can be thought of as "us versus them." It starts with "I'm not sure I want those people [(that you mention)." This sets up a reference structure in which "you and I" are talking about "them." In lines 3 and 6 and again at line 16, David tries to break in with a related but distracting question, which succeeds at line 21 in redirecting the talk. His question is phrased in terms "you," as an indefinite second person plural, meaning something like "people like us." The conversation proceeds then with "I's" and indefinite "you's" contrasted with

61

"them" or "those people." There are two different third person referents: the faculty and other graduate students. This bit of talk positions the talkers between these two groups. The episode is summed up beginning at line 69 by a transition from "you" to "we." The ending then becomes explicit in terms of the identity of the present group and its moral commitments to others. In this set of shifting references, pronouns do very clear work as the carriers of moral claims incumbent on the talkers.

The interaction is structured here not by the topic (integrity and authority), but by the personal references relevant to that topic. While topic can be seen to structure the overall organization of conversational talk (cf. Keenan and Schieffelin, 1976), within topics it is personal reference that organizes the discussion. This is significant, because recognition of this point allows us to see how identity work gets done in talk. It gets done by the speaker creating alignments between people and topics.

Having briefly summarized the episode, I will discuss more generally how each pronoun is used in interaction to create a referential structure that not only satisfies involvement obligations, and in so doing anchors the talk in the moment, but also ties the talk and the talkers to a larger institutional order, as the above comment on moral claims illustrates.

First person singular

This segment of talk begins with a self-referential claim: "I'm not sure I want those people . . . ." This use of "I" fits both the standard grammatical and interactional claims about the role of the first person singular. Not only does it index the speaker, but it anchors the talk in the moment and, by providing a subjective claim, ties it to a previous turn. This use of "I" indicates connection to previous talk, shows a sensitivity to involvement obligations and recipient design demands by stating the speaker's position, which also establishes her footing, and references a category of others ("those people").

This "I" sets up the talker and an addressee as a unit in contrast to another category of people ("those people") who are clearly different from and perhaps morally inferior to "us."[7] Thus a simple claim can be seen to be doing a quantity of interactional work simultaneously.

Quotative "I" Urban (1989) demonstrates that the use of "I" can be referentially more complex than this situation suggests. Urban's analysis of direct and indirect quotation shows how "I" is often used as a referent not to the speaker but to what he calls an "I of discourse." This quotative "I" includes what Goffman means by "say-fors" or mimicry, in which a speaker will make an utterance as another person. In a "say-for" "an individual acts out – typically in a mannered voice – someone not himself, someone who may or may not be present" (Goffman, 1974, p. 534). While say-fors can be referentially problematic, there seem to be fairly clear syntactic and/or prosodic markers which tell hearers "who" is speaking. The speaker may say "She said" or may change from a normal to a marked voice quality to indicate that a different "person" is doing the speaking. Frequently both of these devices are employed simultaneously.

This is what Rich does in example 3.2 when he claims that Pat has not been talking and then says:

Example 3.2

1	Rich:	Now let <u>me</u> address. Let <u>me</u> address. Let <u>me</u>
2		address an issue. If <u>we</u>. If <u>we</u> think (this)
3		Look. Everybody in this room is talk. Except
4		except <u>you</u> {Pat} who are sorta hiding. "<u>I</u>'m
5		hiding in this thing." {Rich mimics Pat}
6		Everybody else in this room is talking as if
7		as if =
8	Kathy:	= Well so <u>she</u> needn't <u>she's</u> not necessarily
9		hiding. Maybe <u>she</u> just doesn't have anything
10		ta say at this point.
11	Amy:	(That's) =
12	Rich:	= Oh <u>she's</u> been scowling periodically.

63

We may assume Rich's use of "me" (line 1) is self-referential, that it refers to the speaker or animator of those words. However, his use of "I" (line 4) is clearly not self-referential, it is a say-for, a piece of mimicry. It is part of an embedded quote, in which he is mimicking another speaker. In Levinson's formulation, Rich is an "author," and also acts as a "ghostee," in the sense that he appears to be speaking for someone else.

It is clear to participants, as Kathy's defense of Pat indicates (lines 8–10), that the "I" Rich uses in this utterance is not self-referential, but is rather a mimicry of Pat. He is, in effect, taking a turn for her, a turn which confirms his claim. It is useful to remember that speaking in this kind of capacity dramatizes a point the speaker wishes to make, by providing an explicit character-ization of someone referred to. The "I" becomes a "figure," in Goffman's sense, of the speaker's utterance.

The first person singular, then, can be interactionally more complex than the self-referentiality of the grammatical paradigm suggests. It is a resource that speakers can use to do a variety of interactional work, including dramatizing others' personae by speaking in an imitation of their voice.

First person plural

The use of "we" introduces significant potential ambiguity into sentences. In English, "we" means "speaker + some unspecified number of others." It can, and often does, include the hearers ("we inclusive"). But it can also exclude the hearers ("we exclusive"). Some languages have separate terms for "we inclusive" and "we exclusive" (Burling, 1970; Lyons, 1968). However, in English, the use of "we" requires the hearer to interpret the speaker's referential presuppositions and intentions in making a particular utterance.

When a speaker uses "we," he or she is assuming the right to speak for the group (see Spiegelberg, 1973) or lecture the group on correct or desirable behavior. In example 3.1, beginning at line 64, Rich changes his footing when he says

68	An I'm saying i'm saying the point is the pi tha,
69	you should, that we should teach graduate
70	students, we should teach graduate students, US,
71	WHAT our responsibility is ta young graduate
72	students

By changing his footing at this juncture on line 69, he no longer speaks as an individual, but as a group member with the group in mind.[8] Thus "we" does important group work in creating and calling attention to identity boundaries.[9]

"We" has shifting sets of referents of greater or lesser inclusiveness, and is a prime example of one of the ways speakers can shift their "footings," creating new alignments with others, in the course of very brief stretches of talk. Because "we" necessarily involves the speaker and statements about who "we" are, it seems to carry an evaluative component to it, which is important for understanding identity boundaries.

For example, in the complete text of the graduate student conversation, "we" appears to have five different referents.

1 We – you (a single addressee) and me. In a discussion about prelim exam results, Amy and Rich exchange the following:

Amy: I could've just as easily done poorly.
Rich: So could I of but we did not.

Rich's use of "we" refers only to how he and Amy fared on the exams. The discussion is over chance versus study in the exams (a topic explored in the second half of chapter 6), and the dispute here is between just the two of them, who compose the "we."

2 We – those of us who are here right now. "We" can also mean "all of us here right now." This usage is almost always indexical to the situation, because by reference to the group which constitutes the event, reference is made to the event itself. At one point, David says: "Can we take a piss break?" The "we" in this case makes sense only as a reference to the group of talkers. David's use of "we" refers to their shared situation at this moment.

65

3 We – senior graduate students. "We" is sometimes used more broadly to refer to "we senior graduate students." In the example discussed above, in a discussion of problems with the department and with sociology in general (example 3.1, lines 68–72), Rich says, "the point is the pi tha, you should, that we should teach graduate students, we should teach graduate students, US, WHAT our responsibility is ta young graduate students . . . ." He uses "young graduate students" as an explicit contrast with the "we" he is speaking for, which is clearly not all graduate students, yet is some group of graduate students who need to take responsibility for socializing "young graduate students." Kathy made a similar reference earlier in the conversation when she said: "I mean we all assume an we we're not we're not like first year students that see all the faculty as one congloberate conglomerate conspiring against us." This identity is one they share with a larger group of people beyond this event.

4 We – graduate students. In this same way, they have an even wider identity as "graduate students." In their discussion of prelim results, Amy says: "An I think that we students. The whole way that that we rank each other according to prelims is absolutely asinine." Amy explicitly says "we students," but the reference is to people who took the prelim exams, thus the implication is "we graduate students," because no one else falls into that category.

5 We – sociologists. Finally, "we" is used to refer to sociologists versus nonsociologists. In a discussion of sociologists' contributions to social criticism, Kathy asks David if there is an interest in social criticism outside the university:

```
1  Kathy:   Is that what they're tapping (1.5) academics
2           academicians outside of the academy ta do?
3           (1.0) Are they tapping them ta be reflective
4           [ta be critical?
5  David:   [Not at all. But I'm saying that w we have
6           the ability ta say things about society. The
7           degree ta which we still accept the the the
8           past constraints on sociology is the degree ta
9           which we are abrogating our responsibilities . . .
```

In another exchange, David complains that sociology is not relevant to the problems American society is facing. He says:

1	David:	. . . society is crumbling and sociology doesn't
2		have anything ta say ta the fact that society
3		is =
4	Pat:	= is crumbling.
5	David:	is crumbling.
6	Pat:	<u>We</u> can't cure it.
7	David:	What?
8	Pat:	<u>We</u> can't cure it.
9	David:	Wh
10	Pat:	<u>We</u> kin describe it.

Both these references to "we sociologists" suggest an ambivalence about inclusion in this group. In the first, it is claimed that sociologists have an ability they are not using. In the second, it is claimed that sociology cannot do anything about the sorry shape society is in.

In terms of the content of the talk, there appears to be a clear boundary between the fourth and fifth referential categories. This is marked by a change in evaluations from positive for the first four to often critical for the fifth. This indicates two different possibilities, neither of which need exclude the other. It may be that "we sociologists" is sufficiently abstract and distant that criticism is not taken as critical of anyone present. It may also be that this use of "we" is the most ambiguous, since these people are still only marginal members of the profession. The "we" used here is a potential "we," and there is some ambivalence about being a part of it or even whether they ever will be.

Because of their systemic (paradigmatic) ambiguity, first person plural uses provide a powerful resource for calling up involvement obligations that require hearers to interpret who "we" are at any moment and hence how and where the interaction is proceeding.

Sacks's and Watson's discussions of "we" and "they" as markers of speaking to or as representative of an organization have already been discussed, and will be mentioned once more in the discussion of third person pronouns below. This use of "we" also illustrates that the word is not a simple plural, but may frequently have a metaphorical reference to a categorical membership.

Second person singular

Second person singular references are somewhat more ambiguous than first person singular, though the ambiguity is usually greater for the analyst than for the speaker or hearer. These references are often accompanied by kinesic cues, such as a gaze or a gesture, which signal which addressee is intended. These may still be ambiguous, but are usually quickly cleared up by an addressee's response such as "Me?" or "Who do you mean?" or the like.

The principal source of grammatical ambiguity is the fact that English uses the same word for second person singular and plural.[10] Thus the number of "you's" being referred to is not always clear. Again, this is the sort of problem that can be cleared up quickly by conversationalists so that boundaries between speaker and addressee are known.

When a speaker refers to a hearer as "you," that hearer is an "addressed recipient," a "target" of the speaker's words (Levinson, 1988). But as Sacks's discussion (see above) makes clear, "you" has a wide range of interactional uses. In example 3.1, the use of "you" to mean "people like us" (lines 53–60) shows how it can overlap with "we," while example 3.2 illustrates its specific use to target a single recipient (line 4) within the context of a generally addressed claim.

In example 3.2, Rich's choice of pronouns transformed Pat from a member of the "audience" ("we") to an "interlocutor" ("you" – an addressed recipient) to an "indirect target" ("she" – an unaddressed recipient) of the talk of the whole group. The participation framework shifted quickly from a claim about "we" to one in which an insertion sequence about a specific "you" winds up derailing Rich's original claim and leads Pat into becoming the object of two other people's talk: a "she."

In this brief sequence, personal pronouns create and re-create the participation framework of the interaction. The speaker's choice of first person plural ("we"), second person ("you"), or third person ("he," "she," or "they") structured the interaction to follow by announcing to all present the particular relation invoked between the speaker and a particular hearer.

Second person plural

The intended referents of the second person plural are even more ambiguous than those of the second person singular. Since "you" may be singular or plural, the person or persons being addressed have to interpret who is included and who is not. The collective "you" has implications for a shared set of characteristics of the addressees. On line 68, example 3.1, Rich says: "the point is the pi tha, you should, that we should . . . ." Here he first uses what can safely be inferred as a collective "you" referring to his listeners, before switching to "we" to more clearly include himself and perhaps to avoid sounding like he is giving orders to his listeners. So just as "we" does boundary work concerning speaker plus others, "you" can also do this sort of work in terms of characterizations of addressees.

Sacks noted that "you" is often used to mean "we" (1992, vol. 1, p. 165, and above). Since it does not have the possibility of excluding the hearer as "we" does, it is useful as an inclusive term. This usage is better considered as indefinite or general, rather than simply as plural.

Indefinite second person

When a speaker uses the indefinite second person, he or she generalizes about experiences that presumably relate to the whole group. Using "you," the speaker makes a generalization about some unspecified addressees in more personalized terms than if a word like "people" were used. When the speaker uses "we" or "you" indefinite, he or she speaks for group experience. As Sacks says, this use of "you" substitutes for "we" and avoids the ambiguity of

69

whether "we inclusive" or "we exclusive" is intended (1992, vol. 1, pp. 163–8).

Laberge and Sankoff (1980) note that the French pronoun *on*, narrowly glossed in English as "one," as in "One should not do such things," is often used in French speech to generalize, so as to avoid the problems of simply talking about personal experiences. *On* frequently replaces other French pronouns, because its use signals intentional indefiniteness or ambiguity and, by so doing, allows assertions of greater generality and in some cases the "formulation of morals or truisms" (p. 280). This is precisely what Pat does with "you" in her utterance: "In other words, it's like getting through this program ta get yur doctorate so you can go someplace an if you wanna teach you can teach. If you wanna continue ta do yur own research you can" (example 3.1, lines 53–7). She has used "you" to make a generalized statement on the nature of reality, rather than one which relates to anyone in particular.

Once again in example 3.1, Rich uses "you" in a general manner. Rich starts this turn with a personal marker, "And see thats like the conclusion I've had to come with in my life" (lines 28–9), and then proceeds to a generalized statement: "is you CAN'T be on the tenure track ya gotta give up the fact that they're not gonna think yur Herbert {sic} Blalock if yur gonna make some statements that goddamn ... matter" (lines 31–6). The "you's" mark positions which refer to "people like ourselves." When Rich says "you CAN'T be on the tenure track," he is referring to young sociologists getting started, the positions these interactants aspire to. When he says "they're not gonna think yur Herbert {sic} Blalock," he is referring to senior faculty members with the power to grant tenure. The discussion has then shifted to an impersonal account of academic life, and then indefiniteness of the referents emphasizes this.

"You," then, has three meanings or ranges of reference: it can refer to a single addressee; it can refer to a set of more than one addressee; or it can refer to an abstract category of people that do something or have something done to them.

Expressions such as "ya know" or "ya see" seem to have this generalized referent more often than a particular one. Schiffrin (1987) says that "y'know marks transitions in information state"

(p. 267), referring to the availability of information to addressees. He calls "y'know" a "marker of meta-knowledge about what speaker and hearer share . . . and what is generally known" (ibid., p. 268). Thus, such an expression does footing work, indicating a shared identity between speaker and addressee.

As the references of pronouns shift, so does the participation framework of the conversation. First and second person referents constitute the actual interaction. The use of first person plurals ("we," "us," "our") and the second person indefinite ("you," meaning one, as in example 3.1, lines 53–60) represent significant shifts of reference within the talk.

Third person

While "I," "we," and "you" connect interactants to each other in talk, "she," "he," and "they" create references to people being talked about, rather than talked to. As both Benveniste (1971, p. 221) and Lyons (1977, p. 638) have pointed out, the third person is very different from the first and second person in that it "does not correlate with any positive participant role" (ibid.). In terms of distinctive features or components, "I" is "+ speaker," while "you" is "+ addressee." "She," "he," or "they" are both "− speaker" and "− addressee." It is, in other words, a category defined by its exclusion from direct address. Since the speaker is talking to the addressee about someone else, the addressee must interpret to whom "he," "she," or "they" refers. There is more paradigmatic ambiguity with these usages, and when third person plurals are used, the inherent ambiguity can easily be exploited by a speaker who does not wish to be perfectly clear.[11]

Third person reference introduces a number of problems. One sort of third person reference relies on the use of proper names for identification. This is not necessarily straightforward, especially since a single first or last name may refer to more than one person. But contextual features − both the range of people likely to be referenced by a particular group of conversationalists and sequential information based on recent reference to someone − go a long

71

way toward narrowing the possibilities of the intended referent when names are used (see Sacks and Schegloff, 1979, on "recognitionals").

Third person reference means being talked about. Thus the speaker creates an object of talk which he or she seeks to describe in a particular fashion. This was seen in the previous example of Rich's characterization of Pat (example 3.2). While this can also be done with second person usages ("Remember when you did *x*"), in that case the speaker must rely on the addressee's agreement and is less free to attribute characterizations or activities to the person discussed. Thus, as we move farther from the speaker, we have both greater ambiguity and greater freedom of attribution.

The interaction in example 3.1 illustrates how pronoun choices can change a participation framework. The episode starts with Amy making third person references to faculty members ("I'm not sure I want those people," line 1). David attempts to break into her discussion with Rich with the use of "you" and "yur" repeated in three different attempts to get the floor (lines 3, 6, 16). Amy and Rich are already engaged in a "you–they" participation framework. Both of their turns involve "they" references connected to personal "you" references ("that you mention," "Don't you see that?"). But once David has managed to get Amy to address his question, the "you" reference becomes impersonally general: "Once you get the legitimate authority behind you, you begin to loose your integrity to a certain extent" (lines 17–18). This "you" refers to "people who become faculty members," not to anyone in particular. The conversation then changes to a more impersonal and abstract discussion with both "you" and "they" now referring to people like us ("you") and different from us ("they") rather than specific individuals.

Rich: And see that's like the conclusion I've had to come with in my life . . . is you CAN'T be on the tenure track ya gotta give up the fact that they're not gonna think yur Herbert {sic} Blalock if yur gonna make some statements that goddamn . . . matter. (lines 28–36)

In example 3.1, third person referents refer to one of two extremes. At one end are faculty, both at the students' university and elsewhere.

1 "those people" – refers to faculty spoken about in a previous episode ("Smith, Johnson, and those guys") (lines 1, 9, 11)
2 "they," "those people" – same as (1) (line 10)
3 "they're" – faculty elsewhere (line 32)
4 "Herbert {sic} Blalock" – faculty elsewhere (lines 33, 38)
5 "their" – same as (3) (line 42)

There is also one reference to "the whole field of sociology" (line 0), which is in other places an indirect reference to sociologists and hence faculty.

The other extreme is references to graduate students:

1 "graduate students" (lines 70, 71)
2 "young graduate students" (line 72)
3 "those goddamn people" – reference to (1) (lines 72–3)
4 "all the students" – reference to (1) (lines 77–8)

There are two other references. The first is to Rich (line 47), where David names him and talks about his problem as an example of the topic at hand. The other reference is to "Somebody" (line 76). Who this "somebody" is, is unclear, but it must refer to something like "someone who is a senior graduate student like us," because it involves "somebody" who talked to the "young graduate students," and it follows a shifting set of pronouns wherein David makes a number of false starts before finally settling on a sufficiently indefinite one to go with: "Well we I We've done it effec Somebody's done it . . ." (lines 76–7).

Except for these last two referents, the interactants locate themselves between these two poles (faculty and younger graduate students), and their conversation uses them as points of reference.

Third person references, then, point to who we are not. They are powerful metaphors for "other." Their use means that "I," "we," and

73

"you" are defined not simply as the people who are present and engaged in this interaction, but, more significantly, as people who are connected to these "others" in particular ways. In this episode, third person identities are ones the participants once had but have grown out of, or ones they may soon have. All present know that "who" each of them is, is defined by that connection.

Sacks's discussion of the use of "they" as a categorical or institutional marker (1992, vol. 2, pp. 182, 291, 391–5) illustrates this point. He first notes how a speaker uses "they" to indicate that she did not engage in a certain behavior. "We went in . . . and they had a drink" (ibid., p. 291). While some people in her group had a drink, her choice of pronouns makes it clear that she did not. Here "they" states a comparison between self and others.

In two other lectures, Sacks develops the idea that "they" is often used not as a plural but rather as an institutional marker. In the first, in a story told about the police, the speaker says: "An there was two p'leece cars across the street . . . and they wouldn' let'er go in" (ibid., p. 181). "They" does not refer to the police cars, but to the police, and "they" is used here as an institutional referent regardless of the number of people who prevented "her" from going in. In fact, it would have sounded odd to say "he wouldn't let her go in," because then the addressee would certainly have had to say "Who?" "They" is understood to refer to a category: the police.

Similarly, in an example already noted earlier in this chapter, Sacks discusses how "we" and "they" are used in "agent–client" interaction (ibid., pp. 391–5). "We" and "they" are used when someone speaks to or "as an agent of some organization" (ibid., p. 391) to signal that it is organizational and not personal identities that are relevant to this bit of talk (see Watson discussion above).

This use of the plural to index an organization both personalizes the interaction by referring to the organization as a collection of people ("they" instead of "it") and distances the interactants by treating the individual speaker as a token of a larger social unit ("we" or "they," not "I" or "he" or "she"). This creativity of usage reminds us of Silverstein's (1976) point that pronouns can function as metaphors for nongrammatical categories such as deference or sex.

CONCLUSIONS

As the analytic philosophers noted with great dismay, words like pronouns lack clear referents.[12] Their referents shift as situations change. This makes it impossible to precisely define words such as "I" or "you," because their meaning is situated. Thus they are irredeemably interactional markers, and their use is ruled by interactional rules primarily and grammatical rules only secondarily.

As Goffman claims, an utterance "opens up an array of structurally differentiated possibilities, establishing the participation framework in which the speaker will be guiding his delivery" (1981, p. 137). In talk, it is pronouns that create this participation framework, and it alters as pronoun choices shift. Interactants are forced to pay attention to these choices in order to understand the shifting alignments, the references, and the involvement obligations they owe to the moment.

The alignments which pronouns create are not merely referential in any simple way. When Amy says, "I'm not sure I want *those people* that you mention . . . involved in any social any kind of social change" (example 3.1, lines 1–5), "those people" is not only anaphoric to certain previously mentioned faculty members, it is also a reference to what Teresa Labov would justifiably call a moral category (1980). It indicates the kind of people that "they" represent.

This is what Silverstein means when he calls pronouns "creative indexes" (1976). While pronouns at one level do the work connecting talk to the situation, at another level, they are creating descriptions of what is going on. Reference to "we" in a clearly inclusive sense makes the speaker and addressee part of the same unit. By contrast, a speaker's use of "you" may separate the speaker from the addressee, or it may be heard as "we," given the right context. A speaker's reference to a co-present person as "she" or "he" or "they" removes them from participatory status in the exchange.

Personal pronominal reference creates the identity coordinates of interaction. These coordinates are not fixed and can shift between and even within a single turn at talk. Their usage reflects the participation status of each referenced interactant, and interaction proceeds within the framework these references construct. The reality of pronouns is the world of the utterance and the obligations it creates.

4

Gender and Talk: Ideology and Interaction

Much of the psychological and sociological literature indicates that male identity tends to stress independence, aggressiveness, competence, and a narrow range of emotional expression; while female identity emphasizes sympathy, nurturance, cooperation, friendliness, vicarious achievement, dependency, timidity, and emotionality (see Chodorow, 1978; Gilligan, 1982; Lipman-Blumen, 1984; Maccoby and Jacklin, 1974; Rubin, 1983; Tavris and Wade, 1984).

When gender is studied in the fine-grained detail provided by interactional sociolinguistic research, the differences are not as easy to stereotype. Aries (1976), in research with experimental groups, finds more overlapping of gender styles and less sex-role stereotyped behavior with mixed sex groups than is reported for single sex groups. M. Goodwin (1993) finds that both boys and girls engage in disputes and confrontations, but that these activities are carried out differently and take place in differently organized social structures. In Edelsky's (1993) study of talk in a faculty committee, both women and men "joked, argued, directed, and solicited responses" (Tannen, 1993, p. 9), but men were more likely to develop a "one-at-a-time" turn or "floor," while women more often engaged in collaboratively built "floors," "where two or more people either took part in an apparent free-for-all or jointly built one idea" (Edelsky, 1993, p. 189).

77

Perhaps the best extended account of this complexity is to be found in M. Goodwin's ethnography of black working-class children's play (1990). She convincingly demonstrates that the girls she studies are as competent as boys to engage in argument and confrontation, and need not display an "ethic of 'care and responsibility' " (M. Goodwin, 1990, p. 284) as Gilligan (1982) claims. Goodwin argues that we must appreciate the influence of "situated activities" (1990, p. 9) on how talk is produced, rather than looking to broad gender stereotypes. My own work also suggests that both women and men are capable of aggressive as well as cooperative styles of talk, even though they are influenced by different gender ideologies (see below, chapter 6, and Malone, 1994).

The simple dichotomies found in the pyscho-social literature represent generalizations based on observations and interviews. They are not so much wrong as simply inadequate descriptions of the reality of actual interaction.[1] What we find when we look at talk is that things are more complex.

GENDER IN INTERACTION

Face-to-face interaction requires the presentation of an identity appropriate to a situation. But it must be consistent with a history of other presentations before the same audiences, and consistent with some internal self-concept of who one is. Hence interaction involves both a style, in the sense of behavioral choices whose combination creates a "unifying consistency" (Lakoff, 1977, pp. 222–3), and an ideology, a set of beliefs about how one wants to be understood by others. Gendered self-presentation, then, is subject to both the constitutive demands of the interactional order and the framing constraints of the institutional order (Rawls, 1987). Style and ideology combine in interaction to create a sense of being within and outside the interaction at the same time (Goffman, 1967, pp. 113–36).

When gender identity is presented in talk, it involves both a particular style and a particular ideology (self-concept). Women's and men's presentations are noticeably different. Noninteractionist research leans toward the development of stereotyped dichotomies to describe this state of affairs. These differences were traditionally explained as a result of differential socialization. More recently, feminist and feminist-influenced scholarship have emphasized how power differences, the sexual division of labor, and different gender cultures all provide more sophisticated explanations than just differential treatment of girls and boys (Chodorow, 1978; Rubin, 1983; Tavris and Wade, 1984). But when interactional data are ignored, the complexity of these differences, the situatedness of the displays, and the presence of overlap in styles are missed.

This noninteractionist research allows us to begin to understand how the self-presentation of gender is framed by features of the institutional order like work, family, romance, and friendship. These institutional structures create a gendered self concept ideology that constrains but does not create the interactional style.

West and Fenstermaker (1995), as well as West and Zimmerman (1987), offer an ethnomethodologically informed concept of gender that goes beyond these institutional approaches by recognizing both the interactional and institutional nature of the production of gender. They point out that gender is not usefully understood as a role, because it has "no particular setting or organizational context" (West and Fenstermaker, 1995, p. 18) within which it is appropriately enacted. Rather, gender is "omnirelevant," to use Garfinkel's term (1967, p. 118), to individuals and their interactions.

West and Fenstermaker define gender as "an emergent property of social situations: both an outcome of and a rationale for various social arrangements and a means of justifying one of the most fundamental divisions of society" (1995, p. 9). This ethnomethodological perspective emphasizes that gender is produced in interaction, that its reality is the encounter in which people come together and present selves. But, as was argued in chapter 1, interactional style is subject first to the demands of self-presentation, whose ends are "the creation and maintenance of self and meaning" (Rawls, 1987, p. 143). Gender presentation, then, must bow to those demands while reflecting the constraints of an ideology that specifies appropriate "gender displays" (Goffman, 1976). An adequate understanding of the effects of gender on

79

interaction must take into account both institutional forces and constitutive interactional demands.

Gender thus exists both within and outside the interaction order. It is produced in the situated conduct of women and men in interaction. But these social actors bring with them notions of what appropriate female and male behavior are, and such conceptions structure, but do not create, the interactions that take place.

PSYCHOLOGICAL AND SOCIOLOGICAL LITERATURE

The psychological and sociological literature on gender provide fairly consistent findings. But those that ignore conversational data tend to make broader claims about dichotomies than seem to be warranted. I will highlight a few representative pieces to illustrate the variety of approaches taken, before discussing what we find when we look at conversation.

This review concerns only American gender differences; I make no claim about the applicability of these findings beyond the United States. I will review three research approaches. The first, and most psychological, focuses on socialization, emphasizing learning appropriate behavior. The second is sociological, and focuses on the social organization of gender roles. The third addresses gender identity in conversational interaction.

Psychological perspectives on gender

Carol Gilligan's work (1979, 1982) provides an influential founda-tion for current thinking about gender differences. In a brilliant, creative rethinking of Kohlberg's (1981) standard theory of moral development, she suggests that the stages of moral development Kohlberg took as universal are in fact not the same for both genders. Her work shows that boys' socialization experiences lead to a sense of separation and a striving for action and achievement in order to differentiate themselves from those around them, while girls' socialization experiences lead to a sense of continuity, first with mothers, then with best friends in small, exclusive dyads, resulting in what Gilligan terms a morality of responsibility which stresses sensitivity to others and worry over inflicting hurt. By contrast, boys' experiences lead to a sense of individuation and a concern for the rights of others. She poses these as two separate, but equally valid, moral systems. These moralities of responsibility and moralities of rights lead to very different self concepts and hence to different gender-based ideologies which females and males bring to interaction.

Joseph Pleck (1981) also stresses the role of socialization. Pleck contrasts traditional views of a male behavioral model with views of the modern male role. But the differences between traditional and modern behaviors are not so striking as the continuities. The traditional role emphasizes strength, aggression, emotional insensitivity to others and inexpressiveness for self, and anger and impulsive outbursts as the only acceptable emotional expressions. The modern role emphasizes economic achievement and bureaucratic power, interpersonal skills in the direction or manipulation of others, emotional sensitivity and expressiveness but only in romantic relations, and maintenance of emotional control in general.

While Pleck may have meant these as contrasts, they can just as easily be seen as no more than an update reflecting different circumstances. We have a white-collar, instead of a working-class, or perhaps urban instead of "cowboy," model of masculinity, stressing competence, control, and individual achievement focused on success. Physical strength may be less relevant, while assertiveness has replaced aggression. Emotional sensitivity and expressiveness are now acceptable, but only instrumentally, to achieve success in romance. In general, emotional control is still highly prized. Pleck points out that male friendship bonds continue to be diffuse and unemotional. Intimacy is now allowed, but only with women. There are changes, principally in increased interaction with women, which lead to some altered behaviors for both men and women; but for the most part, achievement and control are still of central importance.

Pleck's findings are consistent with Gilligan's two models of morality, with women's emphasizing relations and men's emphasizing rights. Both their analyses explain the male concern with rights and justice. When the most important aspect in life is control of others in order to achieve success, moral concerns need to focus on a set of rules protecting the rights of all the players. But when life involves sensitivity to others, morality focuses on responsibility.

Both of the above studies, which represent the findings of a large corpus of literature,[2] focus on how children learn to be a certain kind of person through fairly direct training. But there are other, more sociological studies of socialization which focus instead on how peer interaction produces sex-role characteristics.

The social organization of gender identity

Perhaps the best known of these sorts of studies is Janet Lever's (1978) work on sex differences in American children's games. Lever found, in her observations of the play of 10–11-year-old children, in her interviews of the children, and in their own accounts in diaries which she had them keep, that girls tended to play less socially complex games than boys. This conclusion is based on rating different kinds of play on a set of six attributes: role differentiation, interdependence of players, size of group, explicitness of goals (clear winner), number of rules, and team formation.

For example, girls' games more typically involved two or three girls in noncompetitive play without explicit rules. This included such games as jump rope, playing house or school, dolls, hopscotch, tag or chase games, and hide and seek. Lever points out that these are low on role differentiation (usually one or two roles only), and only indirectly competitive, stressing turn-taking instead. By contrast, boy's games more often involved teams, clear winners and losers, and rules that had to be adhered to. These included baseball, football, hockey, basketball, and soccer.

Even when team sports were eliminated, 54 percent of boys' games were still competitive, compared to 30 percent for girls. Nonteam competitive games included chess and checkers, board games, bowling, and cards. Lever concludes that these differences result in "sex differences in the development of social skills potentially useful in childhood and later life" (1978, p. 472). Boys learn to deal with diverse members playing diverse roles, to coordinate actions and maintain group cohesiveness, cope with impersonal rules, work for collective as well as impersonal goals, think strategically, interact with clearcut leaders and followers, accept rewards for personal achievement, and experience face-to-face confrontations that require self-control or keeping cool.

By contrast, girls' play is more often what Lever calls spontaneous, imaginative, and free of rules or structure. It involves less interpersonal competition (which, when present, is more often indirect – against a previous performance, as in jump rope), is without leadership positions, and often mimics primary relationships (kin or friends) instead of game roles. Lever concludes that girls develop empathy, while boys develop a sense of their place in a complex social structure.

Once more we see evidence of a socialization process which encourages boys to see themselves as separate from, and in many cases opposed to, others, even when cooperating in teams. Conversely, girls learn to deal with others in ways which discourage competition and encourage a sense of shared identity. Two different views of the social world can be seen developing here. Not surprisingly, one leads to fathers who are interested in control and performance, the other to mothers interested in collaboration and nurturance.

In a study based on interviews with 150 couples aged 25–55 as well as her own work as a psychotherapist, Lillian Rubin (1983) concludes that our gender identities are so deeply ingrained in our sense of who we are that attempts to change intimate relations are exceedingly difficult. Using the psychoanalytic models of the object relations theorists (see esp. Fairbairn, 1952, and Rubin's references, 1983, p. 45) and Nancy Chodorow's (1978) feminist reinterpretation of Freudian theory, she develops a picture of gender difference resulting from our parental attachments.

Rubin concludes that little boys' experience of separation from their mothers and its attendant anxiety produces a distinctive masculine personality characterized by a strong sense of separateness (ego boundaries) but a weak sense of gender identity. By contrast, girls never have to experience the sense of separation from their mothers, and so grow up with a strong sense of attachment to

83

others, as well as of their own gender identity, but a weak sense of autonomy (see esp. Rubin, 1983, pp. 40–64).

For Rubin, it is parenting that makes us masculine or feminine. But the relevant issue is not how parents train us to be male or female. Rather, it is "the social organization of the family," with "the long dependency of the human infant" (ibid., p. 40), and the "fact that a woman, even if not the mother, is almost always the primary caregiver of infancy" (ibid., p. 42), that assures that girls and boys will have different experiences from the earliest age. This experience of separation for boys and continuity for girls makes humans into distinctively gendered creatures.

The four studies reviewed so far provide consistent conclusions about gender differences. They not only strongly support the belief in a clear gender dichotomy; they also provide good theoretical and empirical reasons for why this is found. But they lack attention to a crucial variable in this area. Even though all of them are based on interviews, they treat language as if it were merely a "reflection of thought" instead of "a mode of social action" (Malinowski, 1959, pp. 312–13, quoted in M. Goodwin, 1990, p. 286). The language of the interviewees that leads to the researchers' conclusions is itself left uninvestigated. The communicative situations in which engendered activity is produced are ignored. The following studies examine talk itself as a crucial feature.

Interactional studies of gender

Gleason and Greif's study of adults' talk to young (preschool) children (1983) provides some interesting details about how children learn what to expect from women and men. They found that men used more "direct imperatives," while women used more question forms (p. 148). Men, especially in talking to sons, tended to give orders. In telling stories, men concentrated on "telling an interesting story," while women concentrated on "interacting with the child, asking questions and making sure he or she understands" (ibid.). We could say that men concentrated on giving a performance, women on establishing a relationship.

Gleason and Greif concluded that mothers' and fathers' talk differed on two dimensions. First, fathers were more direct, controlling, and relatively impolite. They interrupted more, issued more orders, and were less likely to say polite things. Mothers let children finish what they had to say, asked questions or used question forms to gain compliance, and used polite formulae (ibid., pp. 148–9). This is a good example of Brown and Gilman's (1960) distinction between power and solidarity. Father talk emphasizes power and social distance, whereas mother talk emphasizes solidarity and empathy.

Gleason and Greif's second dimension concerns the child's abilities. Fathers used a more demanding style with children. They used more difficult words, requested more sophisticated information, spent more time testing the child's knowledge, and more time encouraging the child to display that knowledge. Mothers were apparently so well tuned in to the child's wants and styles, partly at least because of a much greater amount of time spent with the child, that they frequently guessed what the child wanted and rarely challenged her or him to clarify or elaborate their utterances (Gleason and Greif, 1983, p. 149). We might call this second dimension one of performance versus interaction.

These two dimensions, the first emphasizing control versus collaboration, the other testing versus nurturing, illustrate an interesting point about early experiences in gender identity. Through these very different interactions, children get their earliest sense of appropriate male and female behavior. More basic than appropriate tasks or clothing or even interests, we have evidence that gender identities are communicated to young children by the interactional styles of women and men. Gleason and Greif's evidence supports the idea that children learn very early that men are controlling and demanding, while women are helpful and caring, just by the way they talk.

Gerry Philipsen (1975) describes working-class men's talk in different situations. Among the men of Teamsterville, his name for a white working-class section of south Chicago, talk is present in greatest quantity when relations are symmetrical; when speakers share features of age, sex, ethnicity, occupation, neighborhood, and long acquaintance. In this situation, it is appropriate to talk easily and volubly. But in other instances only small amounts of talk are considered appropriate.

When a relation is asymmetrical in terms of power, or when there are differences in the previously mentioned categories, talk is more limited. This is true with wives and children, with bosses or supervisees, and with outsiders to the neighborhood and those of a different ethnic background. Finally, in some situations, talk is not appropriate at all. When there are extreme power differences, when a man's status has been threatened or his loved ones insulted, speech is not appropriate. In such cases, silence, physical threat, or violence are what is called for. Thus Philipsen observes:

> speech is the currency of social interaction when participants have similar social identities. . . . Speech purchases an expression of solidarity or assertion of status symmetry. When a speech surrogate is used, such as violence, it is an assertion of distance, difference or status asymmetry. (p. 18)

For Philipsen, talk is a connector, a sign of shared identity. Silence is used toward superiors, and physical action toward inferiors. The men of Teamsterville live in a hierarchical world, and talk is only possible with that limited category of others who stand on the same plane as they do. With those above and below (or those who are simply different) there is no point in talk, because it would be misunderstood. With those below, it would imply equality, and with those above, it would be seen as presumptuous.

Maltz and Borker (1982) give another example of how talk is part of gender identity. Their review of the literature on talk and gender concludes that the impolite, controlling behavior characteristic of males documented so well by Zimmerman and West (1975), Fishman (1978), and others is an example of miscommunication based on different subcultural rules for communication. They conclude that women's speech is characterized by the negotiation and expression of relationships; by the use of personal and inclusive pronouns such as "you" and "we," by giving and looking for signs of engagement (nods, minimal responses), showing signs of interest and attention, acknowledging and responding to past utterances, and attempting to link one's own to those and building on them. In other words, women's speech is clearly relational, and women are actively engaged in working on relations in it (Maltz and Borker, 1982, pp. 197–8).

By contrast, men's speech is characterized by performances such as narratives and jokes; loud, aggressive argument, and verbal aggression such as insults, challenges, practical jokes, and put-downs (ibid., p. 198); and the "routines of victimization" so well described by Roberts and Sutton-Smith (1962). While Maltz and Borker's contrast is probably extreme, it is consistent with the descriptions of male versus female differences found elsewhere in the literature I have cited. It points to two very different gender-related identities being expressed in talk. Female identity empha-sizes connectedness, sensitivity to others' presentations, and, in general, an attitude of affiliation. Male identity instead emphasizes performance, competition, or individuation.

These three studies examine talk itself as a contributor to, and manifestation of, gender difference. Their conclusions are con-sistent with the noninteractionist literature. They are also con-sistent with the bulk of sociolinguistic gender research. However, the following study illustrates the value of an approach that uses ethnographic/conversation-analytic methods to get at the fine details of interaction. It illustrates that gender difference is more complex than dichotomous.

Marjorie Goodwin's work on 8–13-year-old African-American children in Philadelphia (1980a, 1980b, 1990, 1993) investigates the presence of important differences in talk at an early age. She finds that in play the boys and girls she studied constructed directives differently. "Boys typically used directives that empha-sized the disparity in status between speaker and recipient, while girls used forms that mitigated such differences" (M. Goodwin, 1990, p. 64). Girls' interactions emphasized equality and the "non-hierarchical framework" of their groups; thus "intricate processes of alliance formation between equals" (1980a, p. 173) often charac-terized their play. Boys' directives suggested action for "right now," while girls left times in the indefinite future.

In boys' openly hierarchical groups, orders were given, and insults, challenges, and criticisms were a regular part of their play. This made their play more verbally hostile, but grievances rarely lasted for more than a few minutes; while for girls, gossip, ridicule, accusations, and insults of nonpresent girls led to ostracisms and group breakups which lasted over weeks and up to a month and a half.

Goodwin shows that girls' activities can include confrontations, competition, insults, and argument. In the "gossip dispute" activity Goodwin calls "he-said-she-said," one girl accuses another of "having talked about her behind her back" (1990, p. 190). "The offended party confronts an alleged offending party because she wants to 'get something straight'" (ibid.). Goodwin's attention to the fine details of the opening, progress, and closing of these disputes allows her to chronicle their role in the social life of the group. She shows how a next speaker has to "analyze the structure of a preceding utterance" so that she can "display her understanding of it in order to tie appropriately to the previous speaker," and how the meaning of utterances in the dispute results from "their position within the entire structure" (ibid., p. 224).

This analysis examines the interaction order in action. It shows how the involvement obligations of encounters require interactants to behave in certain ways regardless of gender. Yet it also shows that what is accomplished by these disputes differs by gender. When boys engage in disputes, winning and losing affect "relative rank" (M. Goodwin, 1993, p. 112) in the group. When girls engage in disputes, it is because someone has said something behind another's back that violates "the egalitarian ethos" (ibid., p. 119) of the group.

Goodwin's work shows that if interactional style and ideology are not kept separate, the role of gender in interaction is not adequately understood. Superficially, her findings are consistent with those reported earlier. However, the detail of her work demonstrates that gender structures interaction in a variety of ways. The social structure of the group varies as a result of ideas about hierarchy versus equality. But the presence of equality as a valued object in the girls' group cannot be taken to mean that they always engage in supportive (Maltz and Borker, 1982), cooperative (Gilligan, 1982), or polite (Gleason and Greif, 1983) interchanges. The interactional styles of the girls and boys overlap in significant ways, even though those styles may lead to different outcomes.

The literature reviewed here comes to a consistent conclusion: there are distinctive gender-related identities learned from a very early age and reinforced in talk and peer interaction. American females learn to be nurturing, collaborative, empathetic, and non-directive. Their social groups stress egalitarianism, but this is made possible by keeping them small and exclusive. These small, exclusive, emotionally intimate groups tend to be characterized by a certain fragility, and regularly break up and re-form with new members. The emphasis on equality means that everyone is as good as everyone else, but it also means that managerial skills are not as well developed as collaborative skills.

American males tend to be competitive, aggressive, independent, and emotionally insensitive. Their social groups tend to be large and hierarchical, so they learn how to be both leaders and followers. Large hierarchical groups discourage emotional intimacy, but put a premium on social management abilities. American males are likely to see the world as divided into superiors, inferiors, and equals. American females are likely to treat most of those with whom they interact as equals.

This is a neat dichotomy. It accounts for much of what we observe with regard to female–male differences. It gives us a satisfying explanation for the frequency of female–male miscommunication (see Tannen, 1990). It even suggests how social arrangements might be changed to reduce tensions and misunderstandings between the sexes. But when research focuses on the micro mechanisms of interaction, by examining talk itself and what it accomplishes, we see a more complicated picture of gender.

The analysis of conversation in its various forms provides us with a kind of fine-grained observation not available from other sources. We find that in closely examined conversations, this neat male–female dichotomy tends to break down. In fact, looking at conversation on a microscopic level leads to a recognition that interactional style and gender ideology, while they may co-occur, are separate concepts.[3]

ANALYSIS

In the following section, I will show how talkers bring gender ideology with them to interaction, while the interactive styles are to some extent chosen as the situation demands, and how males and females possess and are capable of using both individuating and affiliating styles.

Gender is a complex interaction of beliefs and interactional demands. These two orders are connected by the history of interactional practices. In the case of gender, the "primarily sex-separate peer interaction during childhood" (Tannen, 1993, p. 5) leads to distinctive styles and ideologies. But as Ochs says, "the relation between language and gender is not a simple straightforward mapping of linguistic form to social meaning of gender" (1992, pp. 336–7). The contexts of interaction have their own force, as Goffman, the conversation analysts, and Rawls demonstrate. We should not disregard the overwhelmingly consistent findings of the literature on different gender ideologies. But we must connect them up to interaction, and understand how each influences the other.

The first example is analyzed more closely in chapter 6, but its main outlines can be quickly summarized here. In a dispute over the significance of a shared event in the lives of the talkers, graduate prelim exams, we can detect two lines of argument that reflect stereotypic gendered beliefs. The poles of the argument are individuation versus affiliation, or truth versus chance. Regardless of how they are characterized, they reflect very nicely the positions articulated in much of the literature on gender identity. As Carol Gilligan argues, the male position turns on individual achievement and the right to be recognized for it. The female position argues that all those involved in the conversation deserve to be treated as equals, and that achievement differences between them are a result of chance.

In the following excerpt from the discussion, Amy argues with Rich that his success on the exams is the result of chance: the fact that he happened to prepare for the questions they asked that day.

Rich finds this claim belittling of the work he did to prepare for these exams. He claims his success was due to the fact that he worked hard and wrote "the truth" on those exams.

Example 4.1

1	Amy:	Say what's that TRUTH? What's that bullshit?
2	Rich:	It's the way it's put out. It's the form of the
3		words [is the truth
4	?:	[Yeah
5	Rich:	It has nothing to do with bullshit. It has to
6		do with the ability to say "This is how it is"
7		and say it where they've never thought about
8		it [and and then they see it as the truth
9	Amy:	[Oh Come on Ri:::ch
10	Rich:	You don't believe that?
11	Amy:	No:::o
12	Rich:	Oh (well) man . . . neither do you?
13	Amy:	(I think) its called cha:nce
14	(3.0)	
15	?:	Wait
16	Rich:	Oh you can't put those things to . . . I won't I
17		won't I won't allow that. You rob me of status
18		if you put those things down to chance.
19	Amy:	I don't think we all deserve any more status
20		less than or greater than the other.

There seem to be two accounts of the same event being presented here. Barbara Johnstone (1993) contrasts the different worlds created by male and female narratives. She claims that men's stories are about contests, physical or verbal contests with other people or contests with nature. By contrast, women's stories are about "community or joint action" (p. 69). In light of Johnstone's conclusions, we might see the divergent accounts of prelim exams as two different stories about the same event. In the male version, acting alone (studying) leads to success. In the female version, since we are all equal, success is merely a result of chance. Amy and Rich

91

create different social worlds by the stories they tell of their shared experience. Each sees these events in terms of a gender ideology that provides meaning to their experience.

However, when we examine actual interaction, the need to distinguish ideology and style becomes clear. While the content of this dispute mirrors the claims of Gilligan and others, the style is a separate issue. What we see here is that both speakers use a fairly aggressive, combative style. Amy is certainly not any more "polite" (Lakoff, 1975) or attentive to "face" concerns (Brown and Levinson, 1978) than Rich is. Regardless of the content of their talk, of the ideology represented by what they say, the way they say it does not fit with female/male stereotypes based on the literature. The interactional style seen here reflects interaction between equals and the competitiveness of graduate school.

The second example is from a college freshman writing response group (see Tipper and Malone, 1995) in which four students (Emma, Greg, Raphael, and Vanessa) are discussing the draft of a paper by Greg. This exchange took place in April, and the same group of four had been meeting regularly since the previous September. By this time they were familiar with each other and in this and other transcripts their talk moves quickly and fluidly, with few silences and lots of overlaps and contiguous utterances.

Example 4.2

1	Vanessa:	OK Greg, go ahead
2	Greg:	Well like I told you guys coming down I did it
3		on the wrong section of a <u>Hunger of Memory</u>
4		I did it on the education part so I'm
5		[back to
6	Vanessa:	[But what did you =
7	Greg:	= wh I started off with obsession OK and =
8	Vanessa:	= Obsession with studying?
9	Greg:	Ah of being like better than his parents and I
10		was going to relate it ta <u>Educating Rita</u>, where
11		[Rita
12	Vanessa:	[had the obsession with her education =
13	Greg:	= of, because she wanted to be better than the

92

14		people she was around, but as, as you know I
15		couldn't do this.
16	Vanessa:	Why? =
17	Greg:	= So, why cause I gotta [use "Credo"
18	Emma:	[use "Credo" ( )
19	Vanessa:	Oh alright.

As Greg attempts to describe what he is doing (lines 2–5, 7, 9–11, 13–15), he is seemingly interrupted three times by Vanessa (lines 6, 8, 12), who has dominated this exchange from the beginning ("OK Greg, go ahead", line 1). The argument can easily be made, however, that these are not interruptions in the sense of attempts to take the turn away from Greg. They can be seen as supportive overlaps (or, as Sacks calls them, "collaboratives") designed to gain more information about his essay. Lerner (1991) describes a "compound turn-constructional unit format" in which two speakers "jointly produce a single syntactic unit such as a sentence" (p. 441). Here Vanessa inserts questions which direct Greg's utterance in the course of its production.

James and Clarke (1993) point out in their review of the literature from 1965 to 1991 on women, men, and interruptions (p. 231) that the findings are far from clear on male–female differences in this behavior. In fact, the literature they survey (ibid., pp. 234–6) is internally inconsistent and fraught with definitional and methodological problems. However, it is clear that interruptions can be "supportive and cooperative speech acts" (ibid., p. 238) just as easily as they can be hostile takeovers of another's turn.[4]

Many researchers have shown that this simultaneous talk may be supportive and encouraging. Tannen (1984, esp. pp. 71–9) makes a good case for this sort of cooperative overlapping in a discussion of regional styles. Throughout his lectures, Sacks makes reference to "collaboratives," co-production of utterances, and "utterance completions" (see also Lerner, 1991, p. 455, n. 1, for specific Sacks references).

Regardless of the intent of the interruptions – and it seems clear to me that Vanessa is drawing Greg out, not cutting him off – her

93

style maintains her control of the exchange. Greg's turns are shaped by Vanessa's questions.

```
3  Greg:           . . . I
4                  did it on the education part so I'm
5                  [back to
6  Vanessa:        [But what did you =
7  Greg:           = wh I started off with obsession OK and =
```

Here line 7 seems to be a continuation of line 5. It can very plausibly be read as "so I'm back to wh(at, where?) I started off with," but in mid-sentence, Greg inserts "obsession" as an answer to Vanessa's "what" question.

When Vanessa then asks for detail about the "obsession," she once again provides a direction for Greg's turn.

This may be supportive or cooperative, but it is also controlling. Vanessa finishes Greg's sentences for him, and in so doing provides direction for the talk.

This example illustrates that interactional style is a separate issue from gender ideology. Superficial examination of the above instance might lead to the claim that Vanessa's style is stereotypically supportive, as feminine styles are claimed to be. But such a claim would ignore the fact that Vanessa's support is very aggressive, that she helps Greg by directing him.

Understanding gender in interaction means appreciating the complex interaction of beliefs and styles, each of which is influenced by different factors. Interactional style is situated in the moment and the relations between the talkers, as well as the omnirelevant demands of the involvement obligations of the interaction order. But talkers bring with them a sense of appropriate gender identity, an ideology of how women and men are supposed to act. Actual behavior is the result of those two forces coming together.

Finally, one last example illustrates that men are capable of, and engage in, supportive interchanges as well. In the episode referred to above (example 4.1) and discussed further in chapter 6, the dispute is concluded by the development of a new consensus. One of the participants, David, attempts to create a new narrative that will include both the conflicting accounts previously presented.

Example 4.3

1	David:	OK. OK but let's. OK part of it is too. Is
2		pre-psyching the exam.
3	Amy:	Uhmhm
4	David:	OK and we all had different ways of pre-
5		psyching [the exam.
6	Amy:	[Yeah
7	David:	Now it's a matter of chance that perhaps or
8		whatever you wanna call it. Let's not [qui
9	Amy:	[that
10		you were able to OK =
11	David:	{raised volume to keep turn} = LET'S NOT put
12		any sort of either positive or derogatory (2.0)
13		term::inology on it. That certain people were
14		more effective at pre (1.5) psyching the exam.
15		OK?
16	Pat:	humph
17	David:	OK. I mean i when it really boils down to it,
18		is, there's a great deal of arbitrarily, trarbi,
19		arbitrariness even if there is some degree of
20		predictability to it. (1.0) OK?
21	Pat:	hhhhh
22	David:	And we're not gonna go to either extreme and
23		say that its a 100% a matter of chance because
24		I know if you took it to a car mechanic they
25		couldn't do it. An but on the ot[her han
26	Pat?:	[There's some
27		comfort there.
28	K or A:	[hmhh
29	David:	[On the other hand. There's not perfect
30		predictability

Over the course of seven turns marked by frequent formulaic devices that mark his claims ("OK," lines 1, 4, 17; "Now," line 7;

and "I mean," line 17), and requests for support ("OK?" lines 15, 20), interspersed with supportive remarks from the others ("Uhmhm," line 3; "Yeah," line 6, "humph," line 16; "hhhhh," line 21; "hmhh," line 28), David carefully builds a new story that seeks to honor both Rich's and Amy's accounts of their experiences. His approach is not competitive; nor does it call attention to himself. Rather, it incorporates other people's positions in a collaborative account of their shared identity. It would be hard to find a better example of a story that "revolve[d] around the norms of the community and joint action" (Johnstone, 1993, p. 69), as women's stories are said to do. Rather than dealing with "contest and achievement" (ibid.), it honors the involvement obligations of the group by assuring that all share the same reality. This is certainly not a description of stereotypic male style. And yet David uses the style appropriately and to great effect.

CONCLUSIONS

I draw an important conclusion from this analysis, one which conflicts with the neat dichotomy of male versus female supported by the noninteractionist literature. It is that face-to-face interaction places demands on self-presentation which go well beyond just sending gender-typed signals. While gender ideology may be fairly fundamental or even omnirelevant, interactional style is likely to be more transient, to shift according to a variety of factors.[5] Hence it may be more fruitful to see male and female styles of talk as the result of an interaction of influences, rather than just differing gender-typed styles.

This conclusion really involves three separate implications. The first is that Americans use both individuating and affiliating styles in conversation, and that males and females are capable of using both styles. The second is that ideology and style must be understood as separate, though interlinked, concepts. Finally, this view asserts that conversation, and all interaction, involves a series of shifting alignments. Gender styles and ideologies, as well as other self-presentational concerns, in particular, matters of face, may dictate interactional movement toward or away from one another. I will briefly look at each of these concerns.

First, strategies of individuation and affiliation are not associated with gender in a simple sex-typed fashion. Rather, both males and females can have command of both. In chapter 6 and above (example 4.3), it is David who begins the attempt at consensus by trying to reconcile Amy's and Rich's disagreements. By contrast, while Amy takes an affiliative position ideologically, her interactional style is as individuating as Rich's. In the writing response group, Vanessa's style combines support and overt control in such a unitary fashion that her interruptions are individuating and affiliating at the same time. Even if the evidence suggests that males are more frequently individuating and females affiliative, this is a statistical tendency rather than a defining characteristic.

This distinction between individuation and affiliation is complicated by a related implication, which is that there needs to be a distinction between ideology and style. The noninteractionist literature conflates these two issues, but they are separate problems. Ideology, or belief about the nature of the social world, reflects learning and socialization, both of which are probably fairly ingrained or fundamental. They certainly affect interactional style, but style is sensitive to more contextual factors as well. For example, Amy's individuating style may reflect the competitive and individualistic demands that graduate school places upon students, regardless of gender. Hence, while she argues that "we are all alike," she does so in an individuating fashion, setting herself off from Rich.[6] Similarly, Vanessa acts out the stereotypical helping female role, but does so by taking charge of the situation.

In any case, style and beliefs should not be confused, and style should not be assumed to directly reflect beliefs. It is for this reason that self-report data, upon which psychologists and social psychologists usually rely (e.g. Gilligan and Pleck), are incomplete because they are not a reliable guide to how interaction actually takes place.

The final implication refers to how alignments are created, maintained, and changed in interaction. Deborah Tannen (1984) has pointed out that interaction involves continuous signals of

97

closeness and distance. She suggests that signals of closeness to others involve both dangers and rewards. Closeness can be a threat to the other, in that it challenges uniqueness or individuality. It can also be a threat to the one who signals it, in that its rejection can be cruelly felt. Yet too great a signal of distance is not possible, because it is a rejection of the other, and if carried too far, there is no possibility of interaction.

Joan Emerson's (1970) account of the delicate interactional balancing act which a gynecologist must perform during a pelvic examination illustrates this tension. Treating the patient too much like a medical specimen, just one more collection of body parts, is as insulting and dangerous as is too much personal, individualized interest in those body parts, which brings sexual overtones to a purportedly "medical" situation. Both extremes, of distance and closeness, threaten the situation and can make it unworkable.

Interaction, then, must always balance both kinds of signals. Shifting alignments which tell the other how "we are alike" and how "we are different" must be regularly employed. For this reason, one kind of signal cannot be monopolized by either gender, even if there is a statistical association of one type with a particular gender.

The study of how men and women conceive of and present themselves can benefit from a recognition that interaction places practical demands on participants which cannot be completely gender-specific. These demands have to do with honoring the sacred preserve of self, yet maintaining that "working consensus," that display of regard or deference to the other, which is necessarily a part of the concept of self.

Similarly, the study of face-to-face interaction is enhanced by an attention to how interactants signal their affiliating versus in-dividuating alignments. The study of social categories – in this case men and women who accomplish these feats differently – alerts us not only to the variety of strategies possible, but to some of the causes of misunderstanding and anger between members of differ-ent subcultures.

Concerns about self-presentation place formidable constraints on how interaction proceeds. People are sensitive to being misunder-stood or misjudged, not so much in terms of what they have to say, but in terms of who they are. Americans tend to present themselves and think of themselves in highly gender-stereotyped ways. This leads to talk strategies that reinforce these differences.

However, when other considerations, such as group solidarity or loss of face, come into play due to arguments or formulations which favor some group members at the expense of others, gender-typed concerns are likely to give way to larger moral issues, such as one's character as a good person. In these situations, the complexity of influences on spoken interaction becomes apparent.

5

How to Do Things with Friends: Altercasting and Recipient Design

Language is not a neutral medium that passes freely and easily into the private property of the speaker's intentions; it is populated – overpopulated – with the intentions of others. Expropriating it, forcing it to submit to one's own intentions and accents, is a difficult and complicated process.

M. Bakhtin, *The Dialogic Imagination*

RECIPIENT DESIGN AND ALTERCASTING

Harvey Sacks invented the term "recipient design" to capture the process of how pieces of interaction are designed to make sense to recipients.[1] The concept of "recipient design" subsumes a large variety of interactional concepts, not only from conversation analysis, but also from discourse analysis and symbolic interactionism. By focusing on how utterances are crafted and employed with a recipient's perspective in mind, recipient design provides a general category which includes "action projections" and "preliminaries to preliminaries" (Schegloff, 1980), "assessments" (Pomerantz, 1984a), "perspective display series" (Maynard, 1989), "personal point of

100

view prefaces" (Stubbs, 1983), "rhetorical argument prefaces" (Schiffrin, 1985), "vocabularies of motive" (Mills 1981), "accounts" (Scott and Lyman, 1968), "disclaimers" (Hewitt and Stokes, 1975), and "altercasting" (Weinstein and Deutschberger, 1963). All these terms refer to how behavior is interactionally shaped; how awareness of and sensitivity to the perspective of "the other" is a basic element of interaction.

When someone says "Let me ask you a question" or "I'd like to tell you something," and the respondent says "Okay," he or she has let him or herself in for all kinds of possibilities. In agreeing to be questioned, one commits oneself to providing or refusing an answer, either of which is likely to reflect the kind of person one is (Goody, 1978). Similarly, in agreeing to be told something, not only is one likely to have to respond in some way, but power relations are being established between someone who knows something and is imparting it and someone who does not know and is being told. In either case, this routine is constitutive of the relations to follow between the interactants.[2]

This "action projection" (Schegloff, 1980) takes the form of a request for permission, but in reality is simply a warning or an announcement. It is not a serious permission request, because the recipient is not provided with sufficient information with which to make a permission-granting or rejecting response. The recipient may respond tentatively with an answer such as "What about?" But most competent native speakers of American English will recognize this routine as something other than what it appears to be formally.[3] What the strategy does is cast the other into an interactional role, the role of assistant to the asker's impending performance.

I am suggesting that the use of this phrase illuminates how the symbolic interactionist concept of 'altercasting' (Weinstein and Deutschberger, 1963) is accomplished. Altercasting can be understood as an instance of such a design.

Altercasting is "projecting an identity, to be assumed by other[s] with whom one is in interaction, which is congruent with one's own goals. It is posited as a basic technique of interpersonal control" (ibid., p. 454). The concept was first offered as the reciprocal of self-presentation. Weinstein saw this ability as explicitly strategic, as part of interactional competence. "Skill at establishing and maintaining desired identities both for one's self and for others, is pivotal in being interpersonally competent" (Weinstein, 1969, p. 757). In order to be interactionally successful, we must be able to get others to act in concert with our own desires. Altercasting behavior would be impossible without a sensitivity to how one's actions affect another. It is its recipient design features that allow it to work. It will also become clear that altercasting involves shifts in footing (Goffman, 1981) or changes in interactional alignments as it proceeds.

This chapter analyzes closely a "perspective display series" that attempts to cast its recipient in the role of supporter of the speaker's proposal before that proposal has been made. It is an incident of altercasting, in which the speaker uses a format "designed for the recipient" (Sacks, 1992, vol. 2, p. 230) to solicit the recipient's opinion in order to present his own.

Perspective displays and preliminaries to preliminaries

Maynard and Schegloff have described methods that illustrate the role of recipient design in a speaker's "manipulation" of a hearer, though conversation analysts might hesitate at the use of such a loaded term. In making claims about some state of affairs or an evaluation of some phenomenon, a speaker is often in the position of making not only a disputable claim, but one which impinges upon the expertise of one or more of his or her listeners. Being aware that a challenge is possible, a speaker may employ a number of preliminary strategies that attempt to pre-empt disagreement in various ways by taking the hearer into consideration even before the claim is made. Previously noted strategies, including disclaimers, rhetorical argument prefaces and personal point of view prefaces, all attempt to forestall disagreement. But these only work when the speaker limits his or her remarks to a personal opinion. In situations where an utterance has an important bearing on a recipient or listener, a more complex recipient design strategy is required, one in which the other is given some stake in the utterance.

Maynard's three-part perspective display series and Schegloff's five-part preliminaries to preliminaries involve this sort of "manipulation." They are the most general formulations of the class of strategies which Schegloff calls "action projections" (1980).

A "perspective-display series" includes a query ("So what do you think of . . .?"), the recipient's response, and the "asker's subsequent report" (Maynard, 1989, p. 91). In this fashion, the asker appears sensitive to the other's opinions, avoids blatant disagreements, and in some cases allows the other to state the sensitive or bad news first (see also Maynard, 1991a, 1991b; Gill and Maynard, 1995). Here is an example from a doctor–patient interaction, in which the physician first elicits the mother's understanding of her son's problem before offering his own diagnosis (Maynard, 1992, pp. 337–8).

```
1   Doctor:   What do you see? as-as his (0.5) difficulty.
2             (1.2)
3   Mother:   Mainly his uhm: (1.2) the fact that he
4             doesn't understand everything. (0.6) and
5             also the fact that his speech (0.7) is very
6             hard to understand what he's saying (0.3)
7             lot[s of time
8   Doctor:      [right
9             (0.2)
10  Doctor:   Do you have any ideas wh:y it is? are you:
11            d[o you? h
12  Mother:    [No
13            (2.1)
14  Doctor:   h okay I (0.2) you know I think we basically
15            (.) in some ways agree with you: (0.6) hh
16            insofar as we think that (0.3) Dan's main
17            problem (0.4) h you know does: involve you
18            know language.
```

Perspective display series are designed "to solicit another party's opinion and to then produce one's own report or assessment in a way that takes the other's perspective into account" (Maynard, 1989, p. 91). By apparently "formulating agreement," these sequences "co-implicate" the recipient in the asker's final statement (Maynard, 1991b, p. 168). This strategy "permits the clinician to assess the recipient's perspective before delivering the news" (Gill and Maynard, 1995, p. 16). According to Maynard, these "inherently cautious maneuver[s]" tend to be found in "environments of professional–lay interaction," and "conversations among unacquainted parties" (1989, p. 93). In both cases, they appear when speakers can take little for granted about their listeners and when the potential for conflict is high.

Gill and Maynard (1995) point out that this strategy allows "footing" shifts by the clinician or questioner in response to the other's answers in at least two ways. Not only can the questioner change footing in response to an answer, in order to appear more agreeable (Gill and Maynard, 1995, p. 18), but even more significantly, this strategy allows for the recipient's co-implication, which results in the appearance of a jointly "authored" response (ibid., p. 16). A perspective display series is a self-presentational technique that establishes interactional alignments by attempting to discover another's position and orient to it in some fashion. It is not a simple seeking of agreement. Rather, it is the design of a turn informed by knowledge about the recipient.

"Preliminaries to preliminaries" involve (1) a request to ask a question, (2) agreement, (3) a question which checks the recipient's knowledge of a topic, (4) a second response, and then (5) movement into the topic of interest to the speaker (Schegloff, 1980, pp. 114–15). In the following example from Schegloff (ibid., p. 133), a speaker asks about what he presumes to be common knowledge, hailing taxis.

```
10   A:        Wai'sec'n. Lemme ask you
11             something.
12   B:        Yes
13   A:        You are aware of how that light
14             works on top aren'cha,
15   B:        We::ll, n- uh I know thet it
16             says 'off duty' when they're off
17             duty,
18   A:        Well did you al-
```

19	B:	An' I know its lit up when
20		they are, <u>avail</u>able
21	A:	When they're empty. Right.
22	B:	C'<u>rrect</u>.

In this segment, the request: "Lemme ask you something" (lines 10–11) is followed by an agreement (line 12), which is followed by a statement checking the recipient's knowledge of how to hail a taxi (lines 13–14). This is followed by the recipient's account of his own knowledge (lines 15 and 19) and A's attempt at line 18 to ask the intended question.

Preliminaries to preliminaries occur when a speaker wishes to open up a multi-unit turn, check whether the recipient shares his or her knowledge about the topic to follow, or wishes to talk about him or herself by first raising a topic "as it pertains to the coparticipant" (1980, pp. 110–31). In all these cases, potentially delicate interaction is taking place. A speaker uses this strategy to avoid the appearance of holding the floor too long, incorrectly presuming a recipient knows something, or violating norms of modesty by engaging in uncalled-for self-referential talk.

Both of these strategies open up multi-unit turns for the speaker by signaling that more is to come if the recipient will allow the speaker to proceed. All this coordinates both turn-taking and understanding between a speaker and a recipient as if by sending conversational traffic signals.

Schegloff points out that there is an essential ambiguity to these routines. While they are intended to introduce some extended bit of talk, recipients are not sure just where it will lead. Nor are they sure that the projected action will be one of checking shared understandings or of introducing a delicate topic. Hence perspective-display series and preliminaries to preliminaries tell a recipient that what follows is marked as other than a complete utterance in itself; but beyond that things are not yet clear. These routines serve prospecting functions in talk, allowing recipients to understand that they will need to wait for later utterances in order to completely understand this bit of talk (Cicourel, 1974, p. 54).

It is this feature of ambiguity that makes action projections relevant to altercasting. Not only are they a series of adjacency pairs; they are also framing devices which, in prefacing a message to follow, provide potential alignments to it. They not only allow talk to continue; they also create the relevant interactional identities (the "footings") which will be enacted in the routine that follows. As they establish the footing of speaker and recipient, they create what Goffman (1981) might have called "moral alignments," ways of relating to each other in terms of orientations to specific issues.

DOING ALTERCASTING

The following analysis is based on a conversational episode in which altercasting is accomplished through a perspective display series that co-implicates the hearer in the speaker's attempt to make a self-referential claim.

Example 5.1

1	Rich:	Let me ask you, Let me ask you a serious
2		question that has nothing ta do with these lights
3		and these cameras and that sort of thing. OK?
4	Amy:	Yeah?
5	Kathy:	hhheh heh heh
6	David:	Can we take a PISS break?
7	Amy:	HEH HEH HAHA HAHA HA HA, a piss
8		break.
9	Rich:	Um, um,
10	Kathy:	Anybody wanna beer?
11	David:	Yeah. Please.
12		{footsteps leaving room}
13	Rich:	I'm fine thank you. How much of that (1.6) How
14		much of the mathematics that you have, First of
15		all tell me the, could you tell me the sort of
16		names of the mathematics. Da ya know calculus
17		for example? Da ya know nonlinear algebra for
18		example?
19	Amy:	{softly negative} unh unh,

20	Rich:	OK how much of the how much of the
21		mathematics that you have had, in your tool skill
22		and also for your minor? Did you have a minor
23		in mathematics?
24	Amy:	in economics?
25	Rich:	Economics. OK economics is uh, All right just
26		hold it at the tool skill. is applicable to the way
27		you theorize? How much of it, How much can
28		you use is what I'm asking of that stuff you
29		learned? Could ya give me a ratio? (2.1) That's a
30		nice thing a ratio (problem)
31	All?	heh heh heh heh
32	Amy:	Sure
33	Pat:	of math ( )
34	Amy:	I can give you a ratio of anything
35		hhh hh hh hh
36	Rich:	heh heh heh heh heh three ta one!
37	Amy:	Well (2.0) I would have ta say that those math
38		models courses were really good.
39		(2.0)
40	Rich:	in terms of modeling? [Yeah
41	Amy:	[Yeah
42	Rich:	OK I would I would agree with that,
43	Amy:	Yeah an it was a nice approach, An it was
44		something formalized that I jus had gotten, kina
45		piecemeal in my sociology courses (2.1) It was
46		just a way ta, It wasn't, There wasn't that much
47		math. In fact the the linear algebra and
48		differential equations that I'd had previously in
49		lower, lower numbered courses was a lot more
50		difficult mathematically (0.9) than those tool
51		skill courses. But they were like they'd give ya a
52		problem an ya had ta set it up. Ya know how
53		would ya study this?
54	Rich:	Yeah. yeah. and that. See that's what I think, see
55		that's what I think if yer gonna make people
56		mathematical sociologists everybody should have
57		that. Anybody that, anybody that's (gonna)

58		should have it. Because those people that, those
59		people that that WE were training last year had
60		no idea. I mean absolutely no idea that
61		mathematics in some way makes a summary of
62		things ya know?
63	Amy:	Yeah
64	Rich:	They don't know like (1.0) your view of, Here's
65		a, here's how I see, here's how I SEE theorizing,
66		mathematical theorizing. Your view of society is
67		NOT mathematical at base. Do you think in
68		mathematical terms in yer head or da ya see it
69		sort of like everybody's sort of playing it by ear
70		and tryin their best ta cope an that sort of
71		thing?
72	Amy:	{quietly} Umhmm.
73	Rich:	OK. So you've gotta make a, You gotta make a
74		cogent summary of some parts of the society.
75	Amy:	Yeah,
76	Rich:	Ya take pieces ya think are important and then
77		FIT those ta the ways that mathematics
78		constrains things. The way the the the the
79		mathematical theorizing goes on. Does that
80		make any sense?
81	Amy:	Umhmm
82	Pat?:	Yeah
83		OK

In this episode (part of the conversation among five graduate students), one of the speakers, Rich, attempts to make a claim concerning his belief that the proper role for mathematics in sociology is to "make a cogent summary of some parts of the society" (lines 73–4). At the time of this conversation, Rich was working on a dissertation that was likely to have been considered marginal by most members of this sociology department. It was theoretical, and focused on interpretive sociology, the sociology of knowledge, French structuralism, and the work of Michel Foucault. In a largely quantitative nontheoretical department, this put him at odds with most of his fellow graduate students. The claim he tries to make ties together his interests with the mathematical and quantitative interests of most of the others. Hence he uses this extended utterance to make a claim about the shared identity of all those present and, in so doing, create a particular footing or alignment.

In making this claim, there is the possibility that he will be challenged by either Amy or Pat, both of whom are more knowledgeable about mathematical approaches to sociology than he is. Since Pat has been noticeably quiet in much of this conversation (see example 3.2, p. 63), Amy is the more likely challenger. Her tool skill in mathematics and her minor in economics make her the expert in this situation. The hesitant and highly mitigated manner in which Rich sets up his claim suggests that he is aware of the possibility of challenge and attempts to preclude it by obtaining, or appearing to obtain, Amy's support for what he is saying, though before he actually says it.[4]

This case has features of both perspective display series and preliminaries to preliminaries. In this instance, the parties are acquainted, but the utterance the asker wants to make impinges on the intellectual territory of another (see Goffman, 1971), so he must first prevent her disagreement (co-implicate her) before he can proceed (Maynard, 1989). It is also an opening for the speaker to make a lengthy personal statement, and by first soliciting the recipient's opinion on the topic, he has opened a turn for his own opinions (Schegloff, 1980). This is a conversation between equals in which no one can acceptably coerce another's support. In the intellectually competitive environment of graduate school, eliciting interactional support can involve potential status problems and hence is exactly the sort of delicate interaction that both Maynard and Schegloff have in mind.[5]

Altercasting gets done turn by turn. The three part strategy involves:

1 an opening (lines 1–3) which frames the topic. Then a question by Rich provides
2 the co-implication (lines 13–30), which is followed by Amy's response (lines 37–53); and finally
3 Rich's claim (lines 54–80).

109

The altercasting relies on three devices or techniques. First, Rich attempts to appear knowledgeable about a subject that is within Amy's area of expertise. In so doing, Rich is implying "We are alike" (Tannen, 1985) and creating a bond of identity between them. Second, by agreeing with her, Rich casts Amy into a certain interactional role – that of his supporter. Third, Rich attempts to reduce the face-threatening nature of his question by using mitigation and politeness markers (Brown and Levinson, 1978), including hesitation, rephrasing, and the addition of unnecessary words and phrases (Ochs, 1979). Altercasting is accomplished through a display of knowledge, agreement, and mitigation.

Without making the stronger claim that Rich carefully manipulates this whole episode (and Amy) for a very specific purpose, it is possible to support the weaker claim that a sensitivity to the demands of recipient design leads Rich to fashion his actions in terms of Amy's actual and expected responses, in order to make a certain statement. Altercasting gets done turn by turn as each interactant anticipates what is likely to happen and how to respond to what has just happened in order to get to where he or she wants to go.

1 *The opening (lines 1–3)* Rich's opening employs a "contextualization cue" (Cook-Gumperz and Gumperz, 1976, p. 20) which is an action projection that foregrounds certain features of the situation to allow the recipient to gain a sense of what is about to come. By providing a context that suggests her answer is important to him, Rich appears to introduce a topic about which he genuinely wants Amy's opinion.

The preliminary to a preliminary (line 1), "Let me ask you," both introduces a topic change (Maynard, 1989, p. 103) and shifts the alignment between Rich and Amy (Goffman, 1981).[6] He repairs the sentence by inserting "serious" to indicate that there is a disjunction with previous talk (Schegloff and Sacks, 1974). By saying "a serious question," he implies "OK, last topic is over and a new one begins."

Then he adds (line 2): "that has nothing ta do with these lights and these cameras and that sort of thing. OK?" He distances himself and this question from the situation as if to say: "I'd be

110

interested in your answer to this even if we weren't in this situation."

It is worth remembering Schegloff's point that preliminaries to preliminaries raise a topic "as it pertains to a coparticipant," so that the speaker is then able to talk about it in relation to himself (1980, p. 131). Here the altercasting begins by casting Amy into the role of someone with knowledge sought by the speaker.

2 *Co-implication (lines 13–53)* This section begins with Rich attempting to ask Amy questions about her background in terms of her skills and her training and ends with Amy's response (37–53). Two features of Rich's questioning suggest that it is being carefully constructed to insure a specific understanding: the use of the action projection, "Let me ask you a question," and the presence of "trouble-spots" (Ochs, 1979, and Schegloff et al., 1977) indicated by frequent repetition, word replacement, and pauses. Ochs notes that these repairs reflect the speaker's search for a "construction that is appropriate to the addressee" (1979, p. 70).

The actual beginning of the altercasting is plagued with "trouble–spots." Rich seems unable to decide just how to proceed. He has a lengthy turn-internal pause (1.6 seconds) after "that" (line 13) and then switches to a clearer referent – "the mathematics that you have" – but stops again and takes a new tack, using a disjunction marker, "First of all," to insert new prefatory material. But even here he gets stuck. "Tell me" is mitigated to "could you tell me." He still seems concerned that he is going to sound too inquisitorial, so he changes the form of his utterance from a command ("tell me") to a request ("could you tell me").[7]

For Rich to imply that he has the right to ask Amy to tell him something or that she is obligated to answer him is an "aggravating" imposition. Reference to rights and obligations is direct and undisguised commentary on the nature of the interactants' relationship and for that reason is open to challenge (W. Labov and Fanshel, 1977, pp. 84–6). Instead, he repairs that implication by rephrasing his request in terms of Amy's ability. She no longer owes him an answer. These recyclings and repairs are signs of mitigation in unplanned discourse (Ochs, 1979).

111

Rich's perspective display proceeds over eight turns with Amy providing only minimal answers ("yeah"; "unh unh"; "in economics"), while he sets up an elaborate question.

It is not until line 26, that he finally gets to the main question and begins mid-sentence, relying on the beginning of the question having been provided in the previous turn ("how much of the mathematics that you have had . . .," lines 20–1): "is applicable to the way you theorize?" But he won't let it drop and give her a chance to answer. He goes on specifying the question in one self-correcting phrase after another for three more lines.

27   How much of it, How much can
28   you use is what I'm asking of that stuff you
29   learned? Could ya give me a ratio?

After a 2.1 second silence, he seems to see how funny that sounds, and mocks his own words by reacting to and caricaturing his phrasing: "That's a nice thing a ratio (problem)," at which point there is laughter, first from a number of people, and then from Amy and then Rich himself. This appears to allow him to give up the floor and gives Amy a chance to answer.

The hesitation and wordy construction of the query may in part be a result of the fact that in this interaction between equals, Rich is trying to get a specific response from Amy but cannot acceptably demand it (cf. Grimshaw, 1980, 1981). Thus he hedges, hesitates, rephrases, and continually pads the request for information in order to soften its potential impact. Maynard notes that this is not untypical of perspective display series which attempt to show that the asker is sensitive to the other's opinions.

Finally, Amy begins her response (lines 37–53), but it is not really in the form that Rich had asked for. His query was phrased in terms of quantity. "How much" is repeated six times (lines 13–14, 20, 27). Then he asks for a "ratio" of how much is useful, apparently to how much is not. But Amy's response is rather in terms of a particular approach that is useful: "I would have ta say that those math models courses were really good" (lines 37–8). Thus Amy has refused, though not necessarily intentionally, to answer in the form Rich has requested. With all the carefully detailed and specified structure of his question, he is still not able to compel Amy to answer the way he wants. We see how difficult altercasting can be, especially when it is between equals.

Rich's strategy of specifying his question very precisely made it clear to Amy that it was an action projection, a setup for something to come. He was asking her this question because he intended to use her answer for certain purposes. He attempted to structure his question in a sufficiently precise way to alleviate her fears of what she might be letting herself in for. The point is that a strategy that appears to limit someone's options may really be designed for the recipient, in that it allows them to see what is coming (Cicourel's "pro-specting"). The questioner seeks to indicate where the line of questioning is going so that the hearer can answer the detailed, subtopical questions in an appropriate fashion and not worry about what those answers are committing him or her to.

3 *Rich's claim (lines 54–80)* Rich responds to Amy's answer by beginning to make the claim that this whole sequence seems designed to have set up. Having raised the issue as it pertained to Amy, he is now free to give his own opinion. He appears to agree with Amy by using an orientational marker, what Stubbs (1983, p. 186) calls a "personal point of view preface" (Yeah. Yeah. and that. See that's what I think, see that's what I think . . .) (54–5).

Here the "that" of "that's what I think" (lines 54–5) and of "everybody should have that" (lines 56–7) does very interesting and perhaps deceptive indexical work. It appears to refer back to Amy's claim that her math modeling courses provided her with a way to think about how to set up a problem ("they'd give ya a problem an ya had ta set it up," lines 51–2). But Rich says something different: that mathematics should be used to "make a cogent summary of some parts of the society" (lines 73–4). I have to admit I'm not sure just what that claim actually means, but it is far less specific than Amy's claim. Whatever it might mean, Rich frames it in such a way that it appears to be supported by, and essentially an extension of, Amy's. By agreeing with what Amy has to say, he co-implicates her in his claim.

Thus Rich finally makes a claim about the role of mathematics in sociological theorizing, a claim which shows that he shares the interests of others in the department, that despite his theoretical and nonquantitative perspective, he is like them. The manner in which he proceeds results in a collaborative answer, but one which has allowed him to control this extended segment of talk and get it to serve as a scaffolding for a point he wants to make.

Summary This episode consists of three clearly marked segments: an opening, the co-implication itself, which includes Amy's response, and Rich's claim. The opening makes an unambiguous conversational transition to a new topic. The co-implication strategically constructs a question designed to elicit a very specific answer, an answer which Rich can use as a foundation upon which to build his claim.

Amy's response, while not constructed in the fashion Rich's question sought (she does not give a quantitative answer to his "how much" question), provides her opinion as well as the grounds for Rich's answer ("that's what I think," line 54). His answer may in fact be seen as a joint construction, incorporating her position into his own (Gill and Maynard, 1995, p. 16). Amy's response illustrates how she has been cast into the role of Rich's assistant. By soliciting her opinion, Rich appears to give her the opportunity to respond as she chooses; yet she is maneuvered into following his lead. Upon her response, Rich is free to make his claim. The outcome is that Rich has controlled the floor over 33 turns at talk and has stated his opinion on a topic of at least apparent interest to the entire group. He seems to have demonstrated his "skill at establishing and maintaining desired identities both for [him] self and for others" (Weinstein, 1969, p. 757) by not only controlling the topic but by getting collaborative support in doing so.

An interesting contrast to this case is a conversational episode analyzed by both Pomerantz (1984b) and Sanders (1991), in which one nurse tries unsuccessfully to recruit another for a home nursing job. This situation can be understood as an instance of failed altercasting, in which the questioner doggedly attempts to recruit her hearer, who just as steadfastly refuses to be drawn in.

Pomerantz's analysis illustrates a series of problems – unclear reference, absence of shared assumptions, and finally simply a lack of agreement (1984b, p. 153) – that lead to the unsuccessful conclusion. Pomerantz uses this case to examine how a speaker "pursues" a response through varying strategies.

Sanders (1991) analyzes this case even more closely, to demonstrate how "goals and plans are potentially emergent and changeable in the course of any social interaction" (p. 168) and how each speaker responds to the other with a series of strategies that appear to grow out of the interaction.

In both analyses, a series of attempts at co-implication are successfully resisted by the second nurse, who provides a variety of accounts which preclude her taking the proffered job. In each instance, the altercasting attempt fails because the nurse who is offered the position refuses to be co-implicated.

SELF-PRESENTATION AND RECIPIENT DESIGN

Erving Goffman once compared the relation of self and self-presentation to the relation between a hand of cards and how the cards are played (1967, p. 32). A hand may be played in a variety of ways, and opponents have only a limited idea of the hand itself from seeing how the player plays it. Each play is a partial result of what cards have already been played and of what the player is planning to do in the long run. Thus some plays may be attempts to get an opponent to play a particular card or see how he or she will react, to fish for information on what an opponent intends. In bridge, such a move is a finesse: an attempt to draw out a particular card by playing one of your own that will force your opponent's play.

Both Goffman's dramaturgical approach (see also 1961b) and Weinstein's concept of altercasting illustrate the mutual construction of a card game and, of course, of any interaction. Not only does one player finesse another, but he or she also reacts to what the other plays, just as the other reacts to his or her play. Each turn

115

is constructed in terms of the previous turns as well as the intended effects it will have on future turns. Interaction is collaborative, and analysis must be sensitive to how each participant provides co-participants with the materials with which to construct the next turn.

Rich attempts to finesse a particular play from Amy, so that he can make a statement he wants to make. He sets up his question carefully, to make it as nonthreatening as possible, since Amy probably knows he is trying to get her to make a particular claim, but not necessarily why; and he could not tell her, because her prior support was necessary to make a successful play. Having obtained an answer from her, though not exactly the one he was apparently looking for, he still plays his card: first by suggesting he agrees with her, hence she supports him, and then by making his claim. But Rich's turn is dependent on the answer with which Amy provides him. That is why he is so careful in constructing his query. In the case of the two nurses, successful altercasting would have resulted in commitment to considerable action on the part of the second nurse. Hence she had far more reason than Amy to resist the altercasting.

Rich has made his claim in a way that co-implicates the support of the most mathematical person in the group. If he had made the claim without first getting her support, he would have been far less likely to go unchallenged, since his statement of the relevance of mathematics to sociology falls into Amy's province of knowledge. While she might not have disagreed with him, she would almost certainly have had to respond, because the others in the group knew this was her area (Goffman, 1971). But instead of letting Amy have the last word on the subject, Rich asks her a series of questions which allow her to state her point of view, and then he incorporates this in his final response. Because Amy was being led, though she knew not where, her answers were brief and somewhat noncommittal. But having given them, and Rich apparently being in agreement with them, she was in a weaker position to disagree with his final statement. Rich finesses Amy into appearing to agree with him. In terms of her role as supporter, this is altercasting. In terms of her specific answers, this is finessing.

CONCLUSION

The organization of conversational talk reveals the self-presentational concerns of speakers and hearers. As Rawls says, paraphrasing Goffman, "the social self needs to be continually achieved in and through interaction" (1987, p. 136). Each interactant is sensitive to the identities of the others, and how conversations proceed is strongly affected by these concerns. In order to make a particular point, in order to be treated in a particular way, and in order to appear as a particular kind of person, interactants must pay attention to the perspectives of the others involved in a conversation. This is accomplished through the recipient design features of interaction. These perspectives are "talk intrinsic" features (Mandelbaum, 1990/1) of the interaction. They are discovered by the interactants, not imposed by analysts.

This analysis has attempted to demonstrate how recipient design structures interaction. Choices of words and phrases, intonation, and the larger structure of the discourse itself (such as question and response order), are all made with a greater or lesser awareness of others' reactions.

Evidence of how recipient design is at the service of altercasting in this episode is found in at least three kinds of devices already noted: shared knowledge, agreement, and mitigation. First, Rich implicitly says to Amy, "We are alike because of our shared interests. We are both concerned with how mathematics is used in sociology, and this line of questions is intended to explore our similarities." Second, this implicit message is reinforced by Rich's agreements with Amy's answers, which will cast her as a supporter of his claim. Third, he attempts to reduce the intrinsically face-threatening nature of a series of questions by his use of mitigation to soften his requests. Because mitigation makes requests less direct and hence less challenging to the recipient, it is part of the larger strategy emphasizing shared identity. Rich's request is mitigated by focusing on Amy's abilities and away from the rights and obligations of the interaction, and by hesitating, rephrasing, and making semantically unnecessary additions. He is careful to mitigate his requests so as not to overtly cast her into a less powerful position, or suggest that he has the right to do so.

Interactionism studies how people construct their behavior so that it makes sense to others. This changes the focus of social investigation from "who does what" (the basic interest of structural-functionalists, conflict theorists, exchange theorists, and even neo-functionalists) to a semiotic one, concerned with meaning. When analysts neglect the study of *how behavior makes sense*, they lose the proper and unique focus of an interactionist approach (Boden, 1990).

Weinstein and Deutschberger asked an interactional question 30 years ago:

> how are lines of action selected and elaborated in Ego's expressive behavior in order to elicit the desired response? . . . just how does he go about the business of getting others to feel or do what he wants them to feel or do? (1963, p. 455)

But to answer this question, they offered a set of dimensions which could be used to describe a particular relation and, by implication, whether or not altercasting was taking place. These dimensions cannot be used as an answer to their question, because they remain stuck in the old problem of "who does what." They never get to the more pertinent question for interaction: how is it done so that the desired outcome is achieved?

Conversation analysis offers the analytic machinery with which to understand just how altercasting and other forms of inter-subjectivity are accomplished. Recipient design is a powerful concept that leads us to understand the skilled work involved in face-to-face interaction, in which interpersonal goals are pursued turn by turn. Goffman's concept of footing and its instantiation in Maynard's perspective display series help to show exactly how altercasting is part of the mutual construction of selves in inter-action.

Conversation analysis's focus on the fine details of talk, including its hesitations, repairs, careful word choices, intonational contours, and sequential development, make it an ideal method for symbolic interactionists to employ to understand just how people are able to "take the general attitude of all others" (Mead, 1934, p. 155). When we engage in a detailed examination of how behavior makes sense to those involved in it as it happens, we begin to understand how interaction works.

6

Small Disagreements: Character Contests and Working Consensus

The value of the concept of the interaction order is that it recasts the traditional tension between society and the individual as one between the institutional and interactional orders. It is useful here because it helps to explain how and why potentially face-threatening character contests result from the tension between institutionally defined identities and interactionally required self-presentations.

Character contests are ritualized competitions in which selves are defined and their boundaries established in their encounters with others. Goffman calls them "border disputes" in the "territories of the self" (1967, pp. 240–1). A "special kind of moral game," they can involve "bargaining, threatening, promising," asking for or giving excuses, proffering or receiving compliments, slighting or being slighted, flirtations, and banter (ibid., p. 240). They are the product of an interaction order which promotes successful self-presentation and attempts to avoid situations threatening loss of face. These features of the interaction order do not have to do with individual motivations; they are structural features of the order.

The disagreements examined here hinge on the self-presentational demands of the interaction order which are challenged by the institutional constraints of relevant identity definitions. The "master identity" (Hughes, 1945) of gender and the role of fellow graduate student provide institutionalized "framing constraints" that are important aspects of the identities which interactants bring with them to the conversation.

A character contest is initiated because gender and role identities provide two of the conversationalists with conflicting accounts of their shared experience. However, this leads to a "run-in" only because of the interaction order's own resistance to face-threatening behavior. As Rawls says, "it is not up to capable agents to decide whether or not to resist institutional constraint. The interaction order resists these constraints in its own right" (1987, p. 141).

CHARACTER CONTESTS

Both Goffman and the conversation analysts assume that interactants honor the self-presentations of others by accepting their identity claims. Goffman proposes that the individual

> tends to conduct himself during an encounter so as to maintain both his own face and the face of the other participants. This means that the line taken by each participant is usually allowed to prevail, and each participant is allowed to carry off the role he appears to have chosen for himself. A state where everyone temporarily accepts everyone else's line is established. (1967, p. 11)

This is a "working consensus," not necessarily a true agreement. It functions for convenience, so that the objectives of the interaction can be pursued without threats to anyone's face.

But a working consensus is not inviolable, and can be challenged when someone believes that their face has been threatened, resulting in a character contest. Challenges occur because "When two persons are mutually present, the conduct of each can be read for the conception it expresses concerning himself and the other. Co-present behavior thus becomes mutual treatment" (ibid., p. 241). We are all exquisitely sensitive to the appropriateness of others' behavior toward our self and to when our self-presentations are being misread or challenged.

The disagreement chronicled here between two graduate students results from a discussion of a shared event, written comprehensive prelim exams. One student's (Rich's) success on the exams has been characterized as due to his ability to "bullshit." When he defends his performance by claiming that his success was due to writing the "truth," another student (Amy) claims that how well people do on exams is a matter of chance. This is a "provocation," because it violates the moral rule that people be evaluated by the quality of their work. When Rich calls attention to the infraction, he gives notice that an offense has been committed. Amy refuses to "give satisfaction" by either apologizing or backing down, and responds with her own moral claim that graduate students should treat each other as equals. In Goffman's words, this pair of turns "together transform retrospectively the meaning of the initial offense, reconstituting it into what is sometimes called a 'run-in'" (ibid., pp. 243–4). The contest has now begun in earnest, since one party has clearly signaled offense and the other has refused to back down.

Gender

The gender-related component of this disagreement contains important interactional features. As we saw in chapter 4, gender should be understood as more than simply a role, because it has "no specific site or organizational context" (West and Zimmerman, 1987, p. 128) in which it is enacted. Rather it is, to use Garfinkel's term, "omnirelevant" (1967, p. 118). It is part of all of a social actor's interactional performances, and in that sense, social action is always gendered. West and Zimmerman claim that "participants in interaction organize their various and manifold activities to reflect or express gender, and they are disposed to perceive the behavior of others in a similar light" (1987, p. 127).

The research reviewed in chapter 4 finds that there are distinctive gender-related identities and ideologies learned from a very early age that tend to be reinforced in talk and peer interaction. These differences tend to predispose females to value affiliative behaviors, while males prefer individuating perspectives. While the differences are more complex and less dichotomous than noninter-actionists claim, because they are subject to the self-presentational demands of the interaction order, they are nonetheless influential. As West and Zimmerman say, "Gender is a powerful ideological device, which produces, reproduces, and legitimizes the choices and limits that are predicated on sex category" (ibid., p. 147). The character contest of interest here results because gender ideologies as well as role expectations come into conflict with self-presentational demands.

Accounts

Rich's and Amy's claims about truth and chance may be variously labeled "vocabularies of motive" (Mills, 1981), "composite devices" (Sacks, 1964), "aligning actions" (Stokes and Hewitt, 1976), or "accounts" (Heritage, 1984, and others). Heritage echoes Goff-man's belief in the mechanics of a working consensus when he says:

> there is a bias intrinsic to many aspects of the organization of talk which is generally favorable to the maintenance of bonds of sol-idarity between actors and which promotes the avoidance of con-flict. . . . [A]ccounts are commonly required as design features of disaffiliative (dispreferred) second actions to invitations, requests and the like because these first actions inherently project affiliative second actions and invoke a variety of assumptions about the desirability etc. of the relevant second actions which, in turn, implicate the "face" of, and the relationship between, each partici-pant. (Heritage, 1984, pp. 265, 272)

Elsewhere, he says that "social actors normally ask for or offer accounts for their actions . . . when some programme of action is frustrated or interrupted or when some untoward action is taking place" (Heritage, 1983, p. 119).[1]

Social actions are "observable and reportable" – that is, account-able – because they are designed to make sense to those who participate in them (Sharrock and Anderson, 1986, p. 57). Social actors are aware of the need to organize their actions so that they are recognizable tokens of the meanings they intend to convey or the actions they intend to pursue. Mutual understanding results from a sensitivity to the necessity of "making sense" to others. Those "sensible" actions include "doing gender" and doing the graduate student role.

But working consensus and the accountable nature of social action in general are an accomplishment, not a given. Repair work is often necessary. What we see here is that Rich and Amy have different accounts of an event in which they both took part. The accounts, in the form of moral claims, only come out when their working consensus is challenged. The accounts that are offered serve as a starting point for developing a new working consensus.

THE CONTEST

The situation

The topic of discussion at this point in the conversation is prelims, mandatory comprehensive written exams in three major areas of sociology: social organization, social psychology, and methods. They were eight-hour open-book exams on a set of questions written by a faculty committee and had to be passed by the end of the third year. The exams served as a major source of evaluation for students in the program. Both faculty and fellow students knew how others had performed, and their opinions of people were affected, though not necessarily simplistically, by these results. Hence the prelims were a source of strong feelings. One conversationalist, David, had dropped out of the program because he felt he could not pass the exams (Malone, 1985).

This segment of the conversation focuses on how people fared on these exams. Because the character contest between Rich and Amy has destroyed the "surface of agreement" that had been presumed, the conversationalists are forced to negotiate a new working consensus: a shared account of the meaning of the exams.

Even without an explicit agenda, the institutionalized role of fellow graduate students calls into play certain expectations about the shared meaning of their experiences. But to explain the dispute between Rich and Amy simply as a result of conflicting role expectations misses an important sociological point. Rawls glosses this in her treatment of Goffman: "the needs of interaction and the social self are a source of consistent social constraint which does not originate in social structure, and which rarely ends up as part of social structure (via routinization)" (1987, p. 138). If conflicting definitions of the graduate student role are not the source of the disagreement here, then what is? From an interactional point of view, the far more important issue is the face threat that results from a challenge to Rich's sense of self and the ensuing character contest which seeks to establish a new working consensus so that interaction can proceed smoothly.

Six segments of this episode have been excerpted here and will be displayed with commentary between them.

Preliminaries

The conversation in the previous episode had concerned changes in the research skill requirements and how the program might broaden its list of acceptable research skills for this requirement. Rich complained that he had had to take computer science courses which were of no interest to him and that he saw this as discrimination on the part of the department against people not interested in quantitative work. Pat responded to this as a criticism of her interests: "it's as if I'm being coopted because I enjoy that kind of thing," to which Rich responds, paralleling her opening format: "I'm being discriminated against because I don't choose your route."

The provocation

The episode starts when Kathy makes a comment which might be interpreted as an attempt to mediate Rich's and Pat's disagreement. She says that Pat has handicaps in other areas, while Rich's strengths are in exam writing.

Example 6.1

```
1   Kathy:   I mean no no no she has handicaps in other ar
2            ya know in other areas [in terms of structural
3            kinds of things
4   David:                          [Right right right
5            right right
6   Kathy:   You can bullshit for 25 pages on an exam .. ya
7            know .. and [get away with it
8   Pat:                 [I canNOT {rising tone to "NOT"}
9            [hmh hmh hmh
10  Rich:    [I only speak the TRUth [on exams hhh hhh
11  Kathy:                           [a hhh hhh hhh hhh
12  Rich:    [I don't bullshit on exams.
13  Group:   [booooo shhhh shoo:::t (for 5.0)
```

Kathy's remark may have been an attempt at mediation, but it is apparently taken as a provocation by Rich. He responds in what sounds like a self-mocking tone, with a slight emphasis on "TRUth." But as the episode's progress reveals, he is very serious: "I only speak the TRUth on exams ... I don't bullshit on exams" (lines 10, 12). It is difficult to say, but Rich's tone might be inviting laughter in Jefferson's sense (1979), though he himself does not laugh until the rest of the group responds with laughs and "boos" and "sh's." Thus Kathy's remark, and almost certainly the characterization of Rich's exam writing as bullshitting, leads to a strong "defensive reaction" in which Rich believes that his "face" has been threatened and feels called upon to "challenge" her remark (Goffman, 1967, esp. pp. 14–25).

Kathy's claim about bullshitting might have been treated as a joke or responded to in kind. However, the urgency of Rich's denial, even though he laughed as he said it, suggests that the remark was taken as a personal insult. This is supported by his remark in line 35 below that this belittling of the exams robs him of status.

Example 6.2

```
19  Amy:     Say what's that TRUTH? What's that bullshit?
20  Rich:    It's the way it's put out. It's the form of the
```

```
21              words [is the truth
22   ?:              [Yeah
23   Rich:   It has nothing to do with bullshit. It has to
24              do with the ability to say "This is how it is"
25              and say it where they've never thought about it
26              [and and then they see it as the truth
27   Amy:    [Oh Come on Ri:::ch
28   Rich:   You don't believe that?
29   Amy:    No:::o
30   Rich:   Oh (well) man . . . neither do you?
31   Amy:    (I think) its called cha:nce
32              (3.0)
33   ?:      Wait
34   Rich:   Oh you can't put those things to . . . I won't I
35              won't I won't allow that. You rob me of status if
36              you put those things down to chance.
37   Amy:    I don't think we all deserve any more status
38              less than or greater than the other
```

The "run-in"

The last two turns (lines 34–8) are at the heart of this dispute. First the participation framework (Goffman, 1981) is transformed. Rich's turn is an "I–you" exchange: "You rob me." It is just between speaker and addressee. Amy's turn transforms the referential structure into something broader. The "we" in "I don't think we" refers to graduate students in general (the anaphora is to "we graduate students," which appeared a few turns earlier). While Rich structures the dispute in terms of what is being done to him, Amy makes a larger moral claim concerning group justice.

The metaphors of the dispute are also interesting, and offer a parallel moral competition. Rich opens with "rob" and hence connotations of theft and violation of his person, his "territory of self." Amy responds with "deserve," countering that Rich has no just claim to what he says is being taken from him, and making a plea for their shared equality. She takes the moral high ground metaphorically as well as pronominally.

But perhaps most interesting is that these two turns offer conflicting accounts of the significance of a shared event: graduate comprehensive prelim exams. Amy (whose exam scores were just as high as Rich's) has suggested that performance on the exams is the result of "chance." This makes Rich's "high passes" no more valuable than someone else's lower scores. But Amy says Rich has no right to (doesn't "deserve") what he feels is being stolen ("You rob me") from him.

Example 6.3

```
151  Amy:    I know people that studied [a lot harder than me
152          and didn't do as well
153  David:                            [What?
154  Rich:   Okay
155  Amy:    And it didn't have any fucking thing to do
156          with how authoritative they are, or how much
157          they knew or how fucking smart they were.
158  (2.0)
159  David:  [Whimsy to a large extent
160  Amy:    [It      had an          awful lot to do with
161          how they felt that day with the kinds of
162          questions [they got
163  David:            [There is a   degree of luck [to it
164  Amy:                                           [which
165  Rich:   [and its unfair
166  Amy:    [an awful lot =
167  Rich:   = I'll admit that but its not chance =
```

Rich's initial self-defense, labeling his exam performance as an exercise in writing the truth, provokes Amy to take the opposite stance and say that she thinks exam scores are the result of chance, and that "It had an awful lot to do with how they felt that day with the kind of questions they got" (160–2). Her response does not offer Rich any satisfaction for the insult he has perceived, and thus transforms the exchange into a "character contest" (Goffman,

1967, pp. 239–58). These claims also shape the argument to follow by setting truth and chance as the poles of the disagreement.

Thus the first 20 lines serve as a preface to the actual contest, which begins with Amy's direct challenge to Rich. Kathy's claim had been more of a clever remark than a direct challenge. Rich began his self-defense by taking a principled, as opposed to a personal, position: "It has nothing to do with bullshit. It has to do with the ability to say 'This is how it is' and say it where they've never thought about it and and then they see it as the truth" (lines 23–6). Thus he offers a description of his exam strategy, which points out why what he wrote was or should be seen as "truth." When Amy says she thinks "chance" is the key to exam perform-ance, the disagreement has taken shape as a dispute between two extremes.

The question of status, which Rich introduces first in line 35, in responding to Amy's claim about chance, shows that Rich has been doubly belittled: both his exam writing performance and his desire to put himself above the others – as Amy presents it – are challenged. This is returned to later when Rich says: "I think you demean me by saying it's chance. I worked hard to get high passes on those exams." Amy does not immediately respond to that, but a few lines later says: "An I think that we students. The whole way that we we rank each other according to the prelims is absolutely asinine." Thus again she refuses to allow Rich to use his high passes as emblems of prestige.

Themes of the contest

The two themes or propositions that run through this episode – chance versus truth and equality versus inequality (status) – reflect the single issue of affiliation versus individuation.[2] This is partic-ularly interesting in light of Heritage's claims that accounts neces-sarily follow "disaffiliative second actions" (1984, p. 272). Amy's arguments that exam results are chance and that graduate students should not rank each other both say, "We are all alike." She argues for affiliation, communion, equality, solidarity, or whatever we wish

129

to call it. By contrast, Rich's arguments that his answers reflected the truth and thus earned him high passes and that for that reason he deserves "status" for those accomplishments, all make the opposite point that "we are different." He is arguing in terms of individuation, agency, inequality, and so forth.

These two positions reflect the purported gender ideologies of female affiliation and male individuation which were reviewed in chapter 4. While the behavior of Rich and Amy fits the gender stereotypes at the level of content, it undermines them at the level of style. Each argues from a gender-based perspective that gives priority to a certain view of people. Amy's approach reflects continuous support for the idea of randomness of events, which suggests a sameness for all people. If events are random, then our individual accomplishments do not make us better or worse than each other.

Rich's approach continually points to achievement and individual action to indicate nonrandomness. But, more significantly and with more threat to group identity, he points to actions which make him better than others.

Amy denies systematicity which would rank and categorize graduate students as being something beyond just graduate students. Rich rejects randomness which would negate the value of his efforts to change his status.

But both Rich and Amy use a combative individuating style to present their cases. Beyond her egalitarian philosophy, Amy is hardly cooperative or collaborative. Nor does David's style, in the following segments, fit the stereotypical male individuating behavior as he attempts to reconstruct a new working consensus. It is possible to argue that the graduate student role, emphasizing assertion and argumentation, provides the interactants with their style. But that doesn't account for attempts at consensus.

The neat female–male dichotomy may not be quite as generalizable as the social–psychological literature suggests. But it is important to note here that two sets of institutionalized identities – graduate student and gender – provide the speakers with conflicting accounts of the meaning of their shared experiences and lead to face-threatening interactional problems which require repair.

CONSENSUS

The argument threatens the "working consensus" of the conversation. As Goffman remarked about maintaining the definition of the situation:

> each participant is expected to suppress his immediate heartfelt feelings, conveying a view of the situation which he feels the others will be able to find at least temporarily acceptable. The maintenance of this surface of agreement, this veneer of consensus, is facilitated by each participant concealing his own wants behind statements which assert values to which everyone present feels obliged to give lip service. (1959, p. 9)

The problem is, of course, that both Amy's and Rich's claims are sufficiently extreme that the rest of the group can support neither and are faced with the destruction of the "veneer of consensus" that had been operating up to this point.

The other three group members respond to this crisis with attempts at consensus designed to incorporate aspects of both positions into a single noncontradictory account.

Example 6.4

458	David:	One's relationship to the prelim really had NO
459		relash had no bearing on on one's sociology.
460	Kathy:	Oh we all understand that
461	Rich:	Yeah [( ) start out saying that
462	Kathy:	[The evidence that that we're trying to
463		gather here is ya know what is it that gets us
464		through. It obviously is not ya know [whether
465		you study a lot ya know
466	David:	[Its not
467		the amount of Its not the amount of work
468		engaged in OK?
469	Pat:	What you read
470	Kathy:	Yeah
471	David:	It's not what you do It's not even really how
472		one writes. It's it's it's an interaction between

131

473		all those things plus whoever's doing the
474		reading.
475	Kathy:	And psycho and your your [your own the way
476		your own head
477	Pat:	[Oh ya mean the
478		exam committee?
479	Amy:	[Plus
480	David:	[Right the exam committee.
481	Amy:	Plus what [questions have to, how many people =
482	David:	[An
483	Pat?	= And your attitude =

The consensus attempts begin at line 458, where David uses his own inability to cope with the exams to divide the relatively concrete aspect of exam performance from the more abstract but personally more threatening or more sensitive idea of one's knowledge or skill as a sociologist. Ten lines earlier, he says:

> That's the other thing. We're using this arbitrary (2.0) criteria, namely prelims and how much one studied for prelims, Which was in bottomline was the thing I never really accepted and the reason I bowed out, I refused to fit, I refused to use that as a criteria for evaluating how much I used, uh, how much I knew about sociology.

This personal narrative, which deprecates the significance of the prelims, serves as the basis for attempting consensus with the claim that opens example 6.4: "One's relationship to the prelim really had NO relash had no bearing on one's sociology" (lines 458–9). This claim is clearly defensive. David is accounting for his own withdrawal from the graduate program, but he attempts to turn his claim into a more general one by asserting that the exams should not be viewed as tokens of one's knowledge of sociology ("had no bearing on one's sociology"). He attempts to reconcile Amy and Rich's positions by uncoupling the putative connection between exam performance and knowledge, and hence their relevance to the argument.

Kathy also attempts consensus, but with a different strategy. She makes a "formulation" (Heritage and Watson, 1980) which attempts to characterize the nature of the conversation as a discussion instead of a disagreement. She says: "The evidence that that we're trying to gather here is ya know what is it that gets us through" (lines 462–4). She formulates the conversation as a cooperative effort aimed at collecting "evidence," not disagreeing. She switches the participation framework to "we" and "us." She also inserts a "ya know," an inclusive discourse marker (Schiffrin, 1987), to further emphasize their shared identity, their affiliation.

This formulation is interesting, because it is not at all clear that gathering "evidence" is what is going on. By inserting "ya know," Kathy appeals to what Schiffrin calls "metaknowledge about what is generally known" (1987, p. 268). Schiffrin defines "y'know as a marker of consensual truths that can be used to seek particular interactional alignments" (ibid., p. 279). This certainly seems to be what Kathy is attempting: a realignment of the group in order to achieve a new working consensus.

Kathy follows this claim in the next sentence with a further claim: "It obviously is not ya know whether you study a lot ya know" (lines 464–5), in which "ya know" "focuses the hearer's attention on a particular bit of information" (Schiffrin, 1987, p. 285). By bracketing the key point, which she suggests they all know ("whether you study a lot"), and including "obviously" as a further indicator that what she is saying is consensual knowledge, she re-emphasizes that they all share this same perspective.

She continues to elaborate, suggesting that getting through the exams is not purely a matter of any one ability, but a variety of abilities, only some of which have to do with study: "And psycho and your your your own the way your own head" (lines 475–6). This turn is hesitant as she searches for the right way to phrase the claim. She seems to be trying to say that each individual has their own approach, but she never makes a very clear statement.

This entire segment is also phrased in terms of the indefinite pronouns "one" or "you" except for Kathy's two uses of "we" and "us." Thus all of this talk is directed generally. This indefinite pronominalization is combined with present tense verbs to give the segment a "timeless" quality, so that it sounds like a general account

133

of how things are, what we all take for granted. The use of indefinite pronouns and the present tense transforms the participation framework so that it displays the attempt at consensus by employing an inclusive style.

After a segment in which Amy claims that Rich was lucky on one exam because he had prepared precisely the material the exam called for, and which Rich cites as evidence of his hard work, we return to the consensus attempt by the other three.

Example 6.5

514	David:	OK. OK but let's. OK part of it is too. Is
515		pre-psyching the exam.
516	Amy:	Uhmhm
517	David:	OK and we all had different ways of pre-
518		psyching [the exam.
519	Amy:	[Yeah
520	David:	Now its a matter of chance that perhaps or
521		whatever you wanna call it. Lets not [qui
522	Amy:	[that you
523		were able to OK =
524	David:	{raised volume to keep turn} = LETS NOT put
525		any sort of either positive or derogatory (2.0)
526		term::inology on it. That certain people were
527		more effective at pre (1.5) psyching the exam.
528		OK?
529	Pat:	humph
530	David:	OK. I mean i when it really boils down to it,
531		is, theres a great deal of arbitrarily, trarbi,
532		arbitrariness even if there is some degree of
533		predictability to it. (1.0) OK?
534	Pat:	hhhhh
535	David:	And we're not gonna go to either extreme and
536		say that its a 100% a matter of chance because
537		I know if you took it to a car mechanic they
538		couldn't do it. An but on the ot[her han
539	Pat?:	[There's some
540		comfort there.
541	K or A:	[hmhh

```
542   David    [On the other hand. There's not perfect
543            predictability because alotta people I respect =
544   Rich:    = on the faculty   couldn't do it
545   David:   Couldn Alotta people on [the faculty couldn't
546   Pat:                             [That's right
547            (2.5)
```

Schiffrin (1987) provides an interesting discussion of the functional complementarity of "y'know" and "I mean" as markers of hearer adjustments versus speaker adjustments in talk.

> Whereas "I mean" focuses on the speaker's *own* adjustments in the *production* of his/her own talk, "y'know" proposes that a hearer adjust his/her orientation (specifically knowledge and attention) toward the *reception* of *another's* talk. (Schiffrin, 1987, p. 309)

What Schiffrin does not mention is how apt this is in terms of gender-marked styles. "I mean" invites hearer attention by a display of speaker orientation, while "y'know" "invites hearer attention and thus directly invites hearer assessment," and in so doing displays speaker orientation (ibid., p. 310). Schiffrin suggests that "y'know" and "I mean" have been criticized by pop grammarians because they reflect "overdependence on the hearer" or "overinvolvement with the self" (ibid., p. 311).

These might be gender-marked conversational styles.[3] While being careful not to generalize beyond these segments, it seems significant that Kathy's consensus attempts rely on the repeated use of "y'know," while David's employ "I mean." Thus even in the consensus attempts which are affiliative in nature, there are gendered ways of achieving the goal.

The participation framework also switches back to specifics here. The "you" in line 522 clearly refers to Rich. In line 526, "certain people," meaning those who did well on the exam, are mentioned. In line 537, "car mechanic(s)" are mentioned, and in line 544 and 545, "people on the faculty" are singled out. The strategy has changed, and now consensus is sought by getting specific.

In this segment, David, in what can be seen as a defensive maneuver as much as a contribution to consensus, alternates claims of agency ("pre-psyching the exam" (lines 515, 517–18)) and chance ("it's a matter of chance that perhaps or whatever you wanna call it" (line 520)), agency ("certain people were more effective at pre-psyching the exam" (lines 526–7)) and chance ("when it really boils down to it, is, there's a great deal of arbitrarily, trarbi, arbitrariness even if there is some degree of predictability to it" (lines 530–3)), and finally concludes with an utterance designed to satisfy everyone, stating: "we're not gonna . . . say that its a 100 percent a matter of chance . . . but . . . there's not perfect predictability" (535–43).

After this conclusion, continuing the argument would be redundant. David's turn at this point redirects attention to how others might do on the exams. The thrust of the character contest has been blunted by David's redirection of the disagreement. Talk has now changed to who could and who could not do well on the exams. Both "car mechanics" and "alotta people on the faculty" are singled out as unlikely to succeed on the exam. Rich's addition of "faculty" to David's suggestion of "car mechanics" maintains some suggestion that in fact chance is relevant. We might say that both parties have emerged "with honor and good character affirmed" (Goffman, 1967, p. 245).

A new working consensus

Working consensus was seriously threatened by two discrepant accounts of the reality that the group had experienced. The first, which focused on individual achievement, threatens to ratify some members as better than others. The second, which focused on individual sameness and the operation of random chance, conflicts with any sense of achievement at all and a shared knowledge (or at least suspicion) that some group members probably *are* smarter than others.

Both accounts are threats to the interactional identities of some group members. To accept either version of reality is to ratify an account of their shared experience which at worst eliminates some members from inclusion in the group and at best establishes a hierarchy among individuals who, as fellow graduate students, are structural equals. This consensus account serves strategic ends by confirming that they see this important event in their lives, prelim exams, in essentially the same way. The new account is a joint undertaking which demonstrates that all of them are sensitive to the complexity of the issue and thus share a single definition of reality.

It is necessary to acknowledge that Amy and Rich never actually formally agree to this new consensus. In the next segment, they come to an agreement on the meaning of the exams, but Amy rephrases Rich's claim so that their agreement is dubious at best.

Example 6.6

548	Rich:	All I'm saying is that the prelims when they
549		existed as a, existed as a place where if you
550		did well on them, you could get a change in
551		the definition of self because the department
552		evaluated them fairly highly.
553	David:	Uhm (2.0) right. um
554	Rich:	I bet on that [because I was on the outside and
555	David:	[Yeah
556	Rich:	did well and did get some of it changed not a
557		lot but some (2.5) Would you admit that?
558	Amy:	Would I admit what? that the faculty look
559		upon (em/you/them?) differently than I do?
560	Rich:	Ye:::ah
561	Amy:	Yeah

Amy's rephrasing of Rich's claim yields a very different proposition from the one he made. She agrees to the fact that "the faculty look upon the exams (or possibly Rich) differently" than she does. This is plainly not what Rich was saying. For whatever reason, Rich accepts her statement, and they appear to agree. From here the conversation moves on to the effects of doing well or poorly on the exams on different members of their cohort.

CONCLUSION

The disagreement chronicled here is about threats to face and the working consensus upon which interaction rests. Brown and Levinson (1978) convincingly demonstrate the widespread, if not universal, force of face considerations on the structure of interaction. In an examination of interaction in three unrelated languages (English, Tzeltal, Tamil), they document the power of face concerns and the seriousness of face threats in face-to-face interaction.

Working consensus is the veneer of agreement which exists to avoid face threat (Goffman, 1959, p. 11). Character contests occur when the normal procedures to avoid face threats fail (Goffman, 1967, pp. 239–58). From a symbolic interactionist point of view, they are problematic, because they require "aligning actions" to get the interaction back on track. From a conversation-analytic point of view, character contests are dispreferred actions because they are disaffiliative. To say they are "dispreferred" is only to acknowledge that when they occur they require a more elaborate resolution than preferred actions (Heritage, 1984). The prolonged attempt at finding an account which resolves Amy's and Rich's differences is evidence for this.

From Goffman's point of view, they are "border disputes" in the "territories of the self," and must be settled if interaction is to continue. This is not to suggest that conflict is normally avoided, or that Goffman's theory of interaction sees disputes as disorderly or as evidence of breakdowns. What it suggests is that disagreements and conflicts are attended to before proceeding to other issues. Character contests imply that the working consensus has been breached and must be repaired before we can get back to the business at hand.

Accounts, then, serve as repair mechanisms. They draw on meanings that are parts of the institutional order. But it is the demands of the interaction order to protect against face threats and to maintain a working consensus that bring aspects of the institutional order into interactional play. As Rawls says:

Some aspects of both language and action have a sequential organization which is not derived from institutional constraints but is instead sensitive to needs of discourse which cut across social and institutional lines. However, every action and conversation takes place within an institutional context of some sort, and this context can always be brought to bear at the level of accounts. (1989, p. 166)

Gender and the graduate student role provide the institutional context for the accounts which facilitate the character contest and for the consensus attempts to resolve it. As sources of accounts, they provide a "vocabulary of motives" with which the dispute and its resolution can operate.

In the intertwining of the institutionalized ideologies of gender and role and the face-protecting demands of the interaction order, we get a sense of the source of this disagreement. The character contest involves both interactional and institutional forces, which in this case reinforce each other.

Perhaps the primary contribution of microanalytic discourse studies is their focus on the real world of everyday lives, rather than the sociologically reconstructed world of interviews and questionnaires. This approach focuses our attention on what people actually do, rather than just on what they claim to do. Both Goffman and Sacks offer a naturalistic descriptive account of the social world that has more in common with both ethnography and ethology than with standard sociology. This sort of close attention to the "methods persons use in doing social life" (Sacks, 1984, p. 21) has already yielded rich results in understanding the interaction order in which selves are created and maintained.

7

Conclusions

Talk constitutes one of the most basic forms of social order in
which human beings take part. It should be at the core of a general
theory of human social organization, one that embodies linguistic
and cultural competence.

M. Goodwin, *He-Said-She-Said*

This study has examined how self-presentation takes place in
everyday talk. It has looked at the machinery of interaction as it
operates in conversation, in order to understand how selves are
created and transformed in encounters with others. In the examination of the fine details of pronoun use, gendered interactional
styles, the manipulation of interactional support, and disputes and
their resolution, we find selves in the social encounters that create
and transform them.

This is the basic stuff of both Mead's "social behaviorism" (1934)
and Schutz's "life-world" (Schutz and Luckmann, 1973), and hence
their intellectual descendants, symbolic interactionism and conversation analysis. It is the minutiae of face-to-face encounters that
provide the evidence needed "to describe methods persons use in
doing social life" (Sacks, 1984, p. 21). We cannot understand how
self-presentation takes place and how it structures interaction by
studying what people say about their behavior in interviews or
surveys, or by what ethnographers' notes describe, or by what can
be culled about attitudes and beliefs from cultural products,
whether written down or enacted. It is the actual details of
interpersonal behavior found in talk that must be studied.

TALK AND SELF-PRESENTATION

More than a dozen years ago, Michael Schwalbe (1983) called attention to the need for sociologists, particularly symbolic interactionists, to look seriously at the interrelationships between language and the self (1983, p. 303). He urged his readers to "expand on Mead's original formulations regarding this relationship" (ibid., p. 291). He provides a sympathetic symbolic interactionist approach to language use. Unfortunately, the path he laid out bypassed the most promising intellectual territory for such exploration.

Schwalbe says language must be taken seriously if sociologists are going to understand the self. He suggests that functional linguistics (Halliday, 1978) and speech-act theory (Austin, 1975) provide the models to which sociologists ought to turn for an improved understanding of "language use as a consequential social activity in itself, not simply as a medium through which social activity occurs" (ibid., p. 299). Paradoxically, he makes no reference to conversation analytic studies of language in use, which at that time already provided over 15 years of research to draw upon, and also provided an explicitly sociological approach to language.

Despite Schwalbe's failure to recognize this research tradition, he calls attention to a central tenet shared by symbolic interactionism and conversation analysis: "for the individual the accomplishment of understanding" (ibid. p. 297) is the basis of joint action. For Blumer, this possibility of joint action is one of the basic features of human social life: "Under the perspective of symbolic interaction, social action is lodged in acting individuals who fit their respective lines of action to one another through a process of interpretation" (1969, p. 84). This issue is central to a social theory that focuses on real actions rather than abstract structures. For symbolic interactionists, the basic research question is how do people "interpret or 'define' each other's actions" (ibid., p. 79) and then proceed to adjust their own actions accordingly. This process is the basis of joint action.

141

But the more basic and empirical question is, How is that interpretation actually accomplished? Neither functional linguistics nor speech-act theory concretely answers that question. By contrast, conversation analysis is centrally concerned with a demonstration of the fact that "linked actions . . . are the basic building blocks of intersubjectivity" (Heritage, 1984, p. 256). This is for the very simple reason that "a second speaker's utterance displays an analysis of the prior speaker's turn and that this permits the first speaker to determine whether (or how) he or she was understood" (ibid.). Conversations, then, allow an immediate display of understanding, or correction in the case of misunderstanding, upon which "joint action" is built.

Not only does this feature (we might even say "essence") of conversation make intersubjectivity possible; it provides "an intrinsic motivation for listening" (Sacks et al., 1974, p. 727). Interactants must listen so that they know how to respond. They must tie their turn to what has preceded it, and then listen again to be sure that they have been interpreted correctly. It is in this simple model of listening that the philosophical problem of intersubjectivity is unraveled. The connectedness of interactants is not the result of "interest or politeness" (ibid.) or other extrinsic factors. Rather, it results from the intrinsic demands of the machinery of interaction, what Goffman calls the "involvement obligations" (1967, pp. 114ff.), that are imposed upon interactants simply by engaging in interaction. Functional linguistics and speech-act theory do not provide a framework that allows this sort of investigation.

It is the work of Erving Goffman and the conversation analysts that provides the approach that allows Mead's interests in language and the self to be empirically investigated and adequately theorized. Such a theory must be able to take account of recipient design, the multi-functionality of talk, self-presentation's semiotic nature, and interaction as a moral order.

The perspective presented here has focused attention on these four intertwined features of interactional talk. Such talk is designed for its recipients. It is structured by the constitutive demands of the interaction order that it be crafted to make sense to those for whom it is intended. The orderliness of interactional talk is not merely a consequence of institutional variables, such as race or age or gender.

There is a more basic social obligation to demonstrate involvement by demonstrating understanding. Self-presentation is an "account-able" activity (Garfinkel, 1967); it is by what we do that people know who we are.

This talk is also multi-functional. Goffman speaks of the in-herent "duality of use" (1983b, p. 4) of interactional behaviors. Body movement, posture, and prosody, as well as talk, have a sufficiently high communicative potential that people regularly convey more than what is uttered. This does not simply mean that people do not control all the meaning that others attribute to their behavior. That of course is true. But it is also true that people intentionally send signals that have multiple meanings, and intend for some or all of those meanings to be conveyed. Human behavior is fundamentally symbolic. Conventionalized head nods or voice inflections or eye movements convey information that accompanies, sometimes supporting, sometimes undercutting, an utterance.

Third, recipient design and multi-functionality mean that self-presentation is best conceived of as a semiotic activity.[1] Self-presentations are, to borrow Perinbanayagam's felicitous phrase, "assemblages of signs" (1991, p. 12), in which information about identity is conveyed in complex, not always intentional, ways. But regardless of intention, we live in (to steal a second useful phrase, this time from Geertz) "webs of significance" (1973, p. 5) we ourselves have spun. Self-presentation is an unavoidable feature of interaction because interactants presume that what is going on has been designed to make sense, yet they know that there is likely to be more information conveyed than just what is uttered. These three features are inextricably woven into our self-presentations.

Finally, self-presentation is a moral activity, along all three of the axes that Taylor specifies (1989, p. 15). It involves a morality of face concerns, both for ourselves, and in "respect for and obligations to others" (ibid.). It also involves our attachment to socially defined goods. Goffman's approach, with its Simmelian emphasis on social-ity, encompasses the first two aspects of these moral concerns. It is Garfinkel's phenomenological attention to meaning, sense-making, and shared perspectives that makes the connection with Taylor's third axis. Lemert (1994) ties the social and the value orientations axes together when he says, "Self definition, thus, is the narrative

143

product of a 'quest' within moral frameworks for a sense of the good in relation to others" (p. 117). Self-presentation is an inescapably moral behavior, because actors are oriented to interactional obligations and are committed to valued goods.

These four features provide an analytic framework for empirical studies of self-presentation. They are features of an interaction order designed to facilitate self-presentation (Rawls, 1987).

SELF-PRESENTATION – INFORMATION, MEANING, AND INTENTION

This concept of an interaction order within which self-presentation takes place leads to a reconceptualization of the issues of information, meaning, and intention in interaction. Goffman's approach to interaction reveals the inadequacy of these distinctions as they are variously employed by philosophers, anthropologists, linguists, and sociologists.

Both Peircian and phenomenological semiotics make a distinction between signs which "intend" to communicate (Peirce's symbols, Husserl's expressive signs) and those which simply inform (Peirce's indexes, Husserl's indicative signs).[2] The anthropologist Gregory Bateson (1972) distinguishes *signs* that are intrinsically connected to what they stand for, and arbitrary, "falsifiable" *signals*. The linguist John Lyons (1977) makes a similar distinction between signals which are "informative" regardless of the sender's intention and those which are "communicative" because they signal a speaker's intention. Lyons points out that information transmission is not dependent on intention, and that what the sender intends to communicate is not always what the receiver derives (1977, p. 33).

Goffman (1959) explodes the utility of this distinction by showing that the contrast between "expressions given" and "expressions given off" has only an "initial validity." The former are signals which refer to "communication in the traditional and narrow sense" (ibid., p. 2). The latter "involve a wide range of action that others can treat as symptomatic of the actor, the expectation being that the action was performed for reasons other than the information conveyed in this way" (ibid.). These "informative signals" unintentionally convey information, such as regional origin or education, by a particular accent. As unintentional "indexes," they would traditionally be assumed to have an intrinsic (indexical) connection to what they stand for.

But because self-presentation is about information management, hearers know a speaker can manipulate both sorts of expressions. Humans are able to recognize that both kinds of information can be seen as what Bateson called "signals, which can be trusted, distrusted, falsified, denied, amplified, corrected, and so forth" (1972, p. 178). In the interaction order, information, intention, and meaning are dependent on the twin demands of self-presentation and sense-making so there are no simple signs. All information transmission between people must be treated as potentially complex.

Because people are generally aware that they are sending more information than they intend, they must carefully package their presentations because of the ever present potential for mishearings. This potential can always be exploited by either or both parties. The putatively unintentional "informational" or "expressive" track, including tone of voice, posture or gesture, may be brought into service to emphasize or undercut the verbal content of a message. Recipients of this information may read it as unintended confirmation or disconfirmation of the message, or as an attempt at cynical manipulation.

In chapter 5, Rich must carefully construct his question to Amy to avoid being misheard. He needs her support prior to his claim, so he cannot tell her what he plans to say. Amy recognizes Rich's question as an "action projection" (Schegloff, 1980). She knows he plans to use her answer, and so is cautious in her reply. The questions and answers are interactionally designed, in part because the multi-functionality of the utterances is recognized.

But this is not to say that we are always in control of all the information that others receive from us. Certainly, accents or expressions may reveal our origins; facial movements may reveal interest or boredom; tone of voice may contradict the content of our words. But since interactants know that this information can be manipulated, that feint and deceit regularly manage impressions, self-presentations are interpreted with a "hermeneutics of suspicion" (Ricoeur, 1970). The rules of interpretation in interaction operate in a context in which not only must intentions be inferred, but the apparently unintentionally informative must be evaluated.

As chapter 3 sought to demonstrate, the choice in conversation of a particular pronoun cannot be explained simply as the result of the application of grammatical rules. Instead, pronoun use itself constitutes information about the relations between interactants. Pronoun use creates a "participation framework" (Goffman, 1981), not an unambiguous structure determined by fixed grammatical rules. Within that shifting framework, interactants create alignments and divisions. They shift footings in response to previous turns, and all must interpret the significance of a speaker's choice for its effects on their "reception roles" (Levinson, 1988).

Because of this built-in ambiguity, self-presentations have what Goffman calls "a promissory character" (1959, p. 2). They are scrutinized for what they might mean and how they fit into the ongoing encounter. They are documentary, indexical, and reflexive (Garfinkel, 1967). Self-presentations stand for or document some other meanings. Since our social actions are crafted to "make sense," "designed for the recipient" (Sacks, 1992, vol. 2, p. 230), they are pregnant with meaning. These meanings are contextually (sequentially) created. They are indexical to the situation, and reflexively create what the situation is about.

An example of the complexity of interactional meanings is found in studying the role which gender plays in interaction, which many accounts drastically oversimplify. Gender identity is a complex resource that includes ideologies of appropriate behavior. But these always come into play in response to interactional demands. As chapter 4 sought to show, there is no simple female or male style. Women and men respond to the sequence of interaction by demonstrating their understanding of events, their mutual involvement. They may then respond in a variety of ways. But it cannot be claimed that men always respond in individuating ways, while women are always affiliative. That may be a cultural tendency, but as we can see from the continuing debate on the nature of "interruptions" (James and Clarke, 1993; Schegloff, 1987b), conversational responses are complex creations, which must first be understood in their productive and interpretive contexts before gender-linked meanings can be attached to them. In the interaction order, gender may be an influential force, but it is not a fundamental one. Gender as a social structure must be "geared into" "interactional cogs" or "filtered" through the interactional membrane (Goffman, 1983b, p. 11). To understand its effect, we must understand how the interaction order "works it into the interaction activity" (Goffman, 1961b, p. 65).

The very act of presenting oneself is the "endless, ongoing, contingent accomplishment" (Garfinkel, 1967, p. 1) that is the basic stuff of interaction. Whether we look at how the indexical meanings of pronouns define "who" is interacting, how gender is reflexively created and re-created in the encounters of style and ideology, how we manipulate each other turn by turn into supporting our claims, or how we settle disputes and maintain a working consensus, it is the interaction order's conjoint demands of sense-making and self-presentation that structure the action. Because interactants know that self-presentations are both meaningful and informative, both intentional and unintentional (as Goffman says, "a potentially infinite cycle of concealment, discovery, false revelation, and rediscovery" (1959, p. 8)), they know that interpretation is necessary.

For this reason, meaning is not something that social scientists attribute to interaction. It is the constitutive property of interaction which is necessary for it to continue. Meaning is inherent in a situation, and can be understood as the interpretation which interactants give to an act and how the original actor responds to that interpretation.

In chapter 6, Rich takes offense at a remark that is not at all clearly intended as such. But regardless of the intent of the original utterance, it is Rich's response that turns the following sequence into a "character contest" (Goffman, 1967), and the dispute must be resolved before interaction can continue.

In terms of interaction and self-presentation, the meaning of an action is the effect it has on subsequent interaction; it is the answer to Labov and Fanshel's (1977) question, "What gets done by what gets said?" (p. 71). As was indicated above, we can study meaning in interaction by studying how second turns follow first turns, and third turns follow seconds. The meaning of a turn must be interpreted for the next turn to follow successfully. Repairs will take care of misunderstandings. Self-presentation then takes place turn by turn as intended meanings and interpreted meanings continuously collide and are reshaped in the interaction order.

If we take conversation analysis and symbolic interactionism seriously, we must turn to interaction to begin to understand how people come to have a sense of who they are and who the others around them are, and of how they are similar to and different from those others. It is in the study of conversation and informal interaction, areas of serious neglect in sociology, that we may seek the processes which develop selves. It is in the informal interactions of parent and child that a self begins to develop. It is in the informal interactions of peers that young children begin to learn how to treat others and how they want to be treated. It is in the informal interactions of adolescents that adult expectations begin to grow. And it is in the informal interactions of adults that new families are formed, decisions are made, and lives are lived. This is not to say that institutional settings are not relevant. Certainly their enablings and constraints cannot be ignored.

Interaction is constrained by institutional demands (Rawls, 1987). The institutional order provides conversational topics, unequal statuses, and different beliefs and attitudes. But all these must be "geared to," or filtered through, the interactional order's constitutive demands for sense-making and self-presentation (Goffman, 1983b). They are "parasitic on an underlying moral consensus" (Rawls, 1990, p. 75) that makes interaction possible.

For this reason, the interaction order is a moral order. It is based on a moral commitment to the "involvement obligations" (Goffman, 1967) that interactants owe each other and to Taylor's three axes of moral thinking: dignity, obligation, and the meaningfulness of how one lives (1989, pp. 14–19). Morality is not imposed by some larger order. Rather, it is impossible to conceive of selves without their connection to moral frameworks which define selves.[3]

In informal interaction, it is conversational talk that directly and indirectly tells others who we are, how we see the situation we are in, and how we want to be treated. Conversational talk is not structured by the demands of institutional decision-making or the professional–client relation or by any demands that a particular direction be followed. It is structured by the demands of self-presentation and the need to make sense. It is just talk; possibly, as Simmel said, "talk for the sake of talking" (1950, p. 52). It is in these routines of "just talking" that selves are created, maintained, negotiated, and changed.

Appendix: Data and Methods

THE DATA

The conversations that are examined here come from a variety of settings. The most frequently used corpus and most detailed analysis are based on two hours of very high quality sound recording and three ten-minute segments of finely detailed film of a conversation which took place among five graduate students of long acquaintance at the home of a friend one summer evening in 1975.

This conversation was recorded as part of the Multiple Analysis Project (MAP) (Grimshaw, 1989, 1994). The project was an attempt on the part of the US Social Science Research Council's Committee on Sociolinguistics to collect sound-image data of face-to-face verbal interaction. Three different events were recorded with both film and audio equipment for analysis by an inter-disciplinary panel of researchers (Grimshaw, 1994). A portion of one of the other events, a dissertation defense, was ultimately chosen as the object of multiple analyses by that committee. The material examined here was officially described as an "*ad hoc* graduate student meeting on graduate student problems" (Grimshaw, 1989, p. 36). There was no agenda and no external constraints on the conversation beyond the participants' knowledge that they were being filmed. The only others present during the recording were two cameramen and a sound man. All names and identifying references have of course been changed.

The second set of data is from videotapes of conversations that took place among undergraduates in writing response groups in a college writing course, where they read and reacted to each others' drafts of class assignments. Once again, students were free to proceed as they chose, but knew they were being recorded, and in this case they had a more specific focus to their talk. There was no one else present during the recording except the response group. They started the video camera when they wanted, and stopped it when they were finished. They were free to turn off the camera during the session if they so chose. Once again, names and identifying referents have been changed.

Finally, portions of transcripts of conversations from the published sociolinguistic corpus collected by other researchers, including M. Goodwin (1980a, 1980b, 1990, 1993), Maynard (1989, 1991b, 1992), Sacks (1992), Schegloff (1980), Schenkein (1978), and Sudnow (1972), are examined for specific purposes.

ISSUES OF METHOD

It is often assumed that recording interaction leads to a sufficiently high degree of self-monitoring that no "real" interaction occurs (see Douglas, 1976). Secret cameras and hidden tape recorders, offered as remedies to this problem, pose ethical dilemmas and can lead to people feeling tricked.

Many researchers have used cameras in institutionalized settings, such as college guidance counselor interviews (Erickson and Shultz, 1982), medical examinations (Fisher, 1982), classrooms (Eder 1982, 1995), or courts of law (O'Barr, 1982). But until recently, there were far fewer "sound-image records (SIR)" of informal interaction. Charles Goodwin's records of conversations in a variety of settings (1981), Corsaro's work on nursery school children on the playground (1985), and Eder's work on lunch table conversations among young adolescents (1995) are some good

151

examples of what is now available. In the last few years, more videotapes of informal interaction have started to become available.

The above work and that described here demonstrate that, when properly undertaken, cameras can record informal interaction and, while not being totally unobtrusive, can provide researchers with valid data on the kind of interaction of which much of everyday life consists. (See Corsaro, 1985, pp. 34–8, for a discussion of the use of videotape recording in natural settings.)

Grimshaw (1989) quotes the visual anthropologist Sol Worth, who "argued that all behavior is 'natural,' regardless of the extent to which it is monitored, and that there are simply differences in degree of monitoring" (p. 66, and *passim* for a discussion of the problem of "monitoring"). It is assumed here – and the evidence of the conversations bears this out – that the "involvement obligations" (Goffman, 1967) incumbent upon interactants force them to attend to what is going on in the talk, or the conversation will simply grind to a halt. Self-monitoring may occur, but conversations demand participant attention, and hence talkers are quickly drawn in, or the interaction fails.

For the graduate students, although there is an awareness of the context, it is arguable that the degree of self-monitoring due to the camera is low. As the evening wore on, and the participants had a few beers, it is hard to imagine that the talk would have been significantly different if the conversation were not being taped.

It might also be argued that a prearranged topic (suggestions for changes in a graduate program) makes for a less than spontaneous conversation. But, as a glance at any of the analyzed sections will show, the topic served more as a springboard for talk than a constraint. The range of the conversation was broad, and while there were occasional calls, by the conversationalists themselves, to get back to the topic, these were not heeded for more than a few minutes. As with most informal conversations among friends, the talk went in a variety of directions, being led only by each participant's contributions and reactions to those. Real conversations flow and, as conversation analysts say, are "locally managed." There was a topic to get things started, but no agenda. This was a conversation, not a meeting.

The writing response groups did not entail informal conversation. They were groups of four or five students who had come together at the request of their teacher to discuss an assignment. The event was structured in the sense that there was some work that was supposed to get accomplished: the reading and critiquing of drafts of each other's essays. However, despite that constraint, these events also lapsed into conversation in many cases, and the change in style from hesitant, carefully chosen critical utterances to relaxed, fluid chatting is easily noticed on the tapes and transcripts. Since these events combine informal conversation with work-related talk, they provide useful examples of stylistic variations in self-referential talk.

Aside from the problem of self-monitoring, there is another issue that affects recorded conversations that is less frequently attended to. The definition of the situation constrains relevant identities in a central fashion (Stryker, 1980).

When the five graduate students were asked to participate in this project, it was as "senior graduate students" talking about their graduate program. This means of defining the situation put them into the position of viewing themselves as "representatives" of the graduate students, and is likely to have had at least two effects on the nature of the conversation.

First, having been defined as "a group of senior graduate students," they were committed in a crucial way to expressing opinions in the context of a graduate student identity. This also probably encouraged the search for consensus on issues under discussion, and perhaps led to the negative reactions to Rich's individuating behaviors examined in chapters 5 and 6. The definition and these reactions may also have contributed to the frequency of Rich's use of indirect strategies to make his points, so as not to overtly set himself off from the rest of the group.

Second, this group identity probably discouraged speaking ill of fellow graduate students. While faculty were frequently "bad-mouthed," other graduate students were referred to in generally complimentary ways. This is not to suggest that in other conversations students regularly "bad-mouth" their fellow students. But having been defined as representatives of graduate student opinion, they may have felt less free to speak as honestly or directly as they might have in other, differently defined settings.

The recognition of this limitation on the self-presentations does not lessen the usefulness of this event as data. It is important, however, to be aware of how constraints external to a conversation, such as others' power to define at least broadly what is going on, can limit the appropriate strategies and contents of the self-presentations.

The undergraduates in the writing response groups were also enacting a particular identity while they were being recorded. They had come together as classmates to help each other edit drafts of class assignments. Although they were alone in the room with a video camera that worked silently in a corner, which they were allowed to turn off if they chose to, they were still in a situation which defined them as "fellow students," not roommates or friends or romantic partners.

While self-monitoring is an issue whose significance has been exaggerated as regards its effects on recorded talk, definition of the situation is a variable that cannot be ignored. However, it does not present researchers with an intractable problem. All encounters provide interactants with ready-made identities (Goffman, 1961b, 1964); the problem is to discover which identities are actually called into play and how they are being used. Schegloff (1987b) makes a very important point when he emphasizes the need "to show that characterizations the investigator makes of the participants are grounded in the participants' own orientations in the interaction" (p. 215). In the graduate student conversation, the conversationalists regularly call attention to their shared graduate student identity in utterances such as Amy's when she says "I don't think we all deserve any more status less than or greater than the other" (example 6.2, line 38–9). In chapter 4, I argue that this line can also be read to reflect a certain gender ideology about equality. That argument is more complex than the one I make here. Here all I am saying is that Amy's claim is explicitly about a "we" that means "we graduate students" and can be heard as a situated identity claim that is about who "we" are at this very moment.

Situated identity, then, is an unavoidable feature of interaction. We interact in situations that have a powerful influence on who we are at the moment. The fact that people are being recorded as they interact does not invalidate the interaction, but investigators must be sensitive to the definitional effect that recording is having.

Single-case analysis

The analyses presented in this book largely rely on what might be called case studies or single-case analyses. Case studies are widely employed in anthropology, but have far less currency in sociology. I believe that the exchange of breadth for depth is worth the sacrifice if we achieve a better understanding of processes that are universal in interaction. Davidson and Costello (1969), Garfinkel (1967), Labov and Fanshel (1977), Schegloff (1987a), Grimshaw (1989), and others have illustrated that these analyses can be a useful method for demonstrating the explanatory power of particular theoretical approaches to interaction.

As Schegloff says, in this sort of approach "the resources of past work on a range of phenomena and organizational domains in talk-in-interaction are brought to bear on the analytic explication of a single fragment of talk" (1987a, p. 101). Schegloff goes on to state a claim basic to all interactional study: "There is a constitutive order to singular occasions of interaction, and to the organization of action within them. This is the bedrock of social life – the primordial site of sociality" (ibid., p. 102).

Labov and Fanshel (1977) claim that single-case analysis allows researchers to "explicate the specific features so that the application of the general principles can be seen" (p. 8).

From a phenomenological point of view, the important issue is our analytical ability to get at the essential features of interaction, not our ability to pile up a sufficiently large number of cases to allow us to claim some sort of statistical representativeness.

Because it is claimed that social encounters are locally organized, that there is an "interaction order *sui generis*" (Rawls, 1987, p. 136), these single events are appropriate as units of analysis, because the organization discovered within them reveals general processes that structure all interaction.

Notes

CHAPTER 1

1 While sociology's attention to spoken interaction is increasing, as the literature reviewed here will demonstrate, it is still a minor part of the discipline. A growing handful of sociologists, especially conversation analysts, would agree with Sacks that "sociology can be a natural observational science" (1984, p. 21; see also Sacks, 1963) and are engaged in work to demonstrate this premise. However, the attention to the fine details of interaction that would permit the development of a rigorously descriptive social science is still absent from most sociological work.

2 This section is especially indebted to the discussions and exegeses of Goffman's writing found in a profound series of essays by Rawls, including 1984, 1987, 1989b, and 1990.

3 Goffman actually uses the phrase "public order" here to distinguish this sort of behavior from that which goes on among intimates, but he is discussing the same topic that he originally referred to in his dissertation (1953) as the "interaction order," which term he uses consistently later on.

4 Hilbert (1992) puts forward much the same argument about the status of ethnomethodology as social theory. He rejects the relevance of the micro–macro distinction as an inaccurate characterization of the relation of ethnomethodology to classical social theory. His discussion in his final chapter (pp. 188–219) provides a useful rebuttal to the reductionism of the standard micro–macro view of social theories.

5 This same sort of distinction is found in a wide variety of sources in both the anthropological and linguistic literatures. Perhaps the best

known is Bateson's (1972) concept of "metacommunication," which refers to the contextual information we use to interpret a message. Blom and Gumperz (1972) make a distinction between the referential functions of language and the social functions. They point out that referential work is impossible without the contextual information provided by the social. Finally, the linguist, John Lyons (1977) distinguishes between communicative (intentional) signs and informative (meaningful) signs. This distinction seems closest to Goffman's. It is discussed further in ch. 7.

6 These assumptions are discussed in more detail in ch. 2, in the sections on Alfred Schutz and Harold Garfinkel.

7 This is perhaps why Gergen (1991) finds Taylor's discussions relevant to his own account of the fragmentation of the postmodern self, because he claims that the social saturation we experience due to today's communication technology makes a clear sense of connectedness impossible. This may be a misreading of Taylor, however, since Taylor claims that identity without connections is impossible.

CHAPTER 2

1 See Gallie, 1966, for an extended discussion of Peirce's philosophical contribution.

2 The influence of Peirce on Mead is not at all clear. The only publication that I am aware of in which Mead refers to Peirce is "The philosophies of Royce, James and Dewey in their American setting" (1964, originally 1929–30). Here he refers twice to "Peirce's laboratory habit of mind" (pp. 385, 389) in terms of its influence on both James and Dewey. In his introduction to Mead's *Selected Writings*, Reck says that "Mead was connected with Peirce indirectly and tenuously" (1964, p. lviii). Significantly (and curiously), in his *Movements of Thought in the Nineteenth Century* (1936), Peirce is never mentioned.

The most likely influence of Peirce on Mead's thinking is indirect, through Dewey's writings, which synthesize Peirce and James. However, Mead's conceptualization of gestures and symbols is so similar to Peirce's use of indexes and symbols that the likelihood of Mead's direct familiarity with Peirce's writings should not be discounted.

3 For a further elaboration of Mead's ideas on the self, thinking, and communication, see Mead's collected essays and lectures (1932, 1934, 1938) and the excellent intellectual biography by Miller (1973), as well as the collection of essays on Mead edited by Petras (1968).

4 The importance of sequence as the basic feature of meaning is central to conversation analysis. See esp. Sacks et al., 1974.

5 Schutz's two most influential publications are his critical synthesis of Husserl's phenomenology and Weber's sociology (1967) and the collection of his essays edited and helpfully introduced by Wagner (Schutz, 1970). Schutz left his most detailed account of a phenomenological sociology, *The Structures of the Life-World*, only in outline form and it was completed by his student Thomas Luckmann (Schutz and Luckmann, 1973). There are also three volumes of his collected papers (1962, 1964, 1966).

6 This is also the object of Wittgenstein's discussion of language-games and the role of language in social life. See Wittgenstein, 1953, 1958.

7 For a concise and interesting discussion of Schutz's contribution to sociology and especially ethnomethodology, see Heritage, 1984, pp. 37–74.

8 For critiques of symbolic interactionism's general lack of attention to social structure, see Giddens, 1979; Gouldner, 1970; Zeitlin, 1973.

9 For other summaries of symbolic interactionism, see Blumer's collected essays (1969), the very fine historical and substantive account by Meltzer et al. (1975), or the essay-length summary by Adler and Adler (1980). For an account of the current situation of symbolic interactionism, see Fine, 1993. For an interesting and eclectic collection of relevant essays, see Stone and Farberman, 1981.

10 The term was invented by Harold Garfinkel to parallel certain studies beginning to attain currency in anthropology in the early 1960s, such as ethnobotany or ethnozoology. These studies examined how the sorts of people typically studied by anthropologists organized and utilized the plants and animals around them, in explicit contrast to Western scientific taxonomies of those same fields. Garfinkel (1974) created a parallel term to label his study of how laymen, as opposed to sociologists, categorize and organize their everyday lives.

11 These principles are variously summarized on pp. 3–4 and 39–42 of *Studies*. They are discussed by Cicourel as "interpretive procedures" (1974, pp. 11–41, 84–8).

12 It is worth noting that this view is not at all inconsistent with Mead's account of time (1932), and especially the notion that new pasts are created by changing presents.

13 For sympathetic discussions of ethnomethodology, see esp. Heritage, 1984; Sharrock and Anderson, 1986; as well as the recent collection edited by Button (1991).

14 For some fairly current reviews of the conversation-analytic literature, see Zimmerman, 1988; Heritage, 1989; Fehr and Stetson, 1990; and Goodwin and Heritage, 1990. Heritage's (1984) chapter on "Con-

versational analysis" is a good account of conversation analysis's ties to ethnomethodology, and Levinson's (1983) chapter on "Conversational structure" is an excellent account of the differences between discourse analysis and conversation analysis, as well as a sympathetic summary of the field.

15 To the best of my knowledge, the first time Sacks referred to this idea was 24 April 1968, when he talked about "how it is that a speaker goes about attending to, orienting his talk to, some co-participant" (1992, vol. 1, p. 765). In the spring of 1970, he refers to a "request format" as being "designed for the recipient" (1992, vol. 2, p. 230). It is not until Fall 1971 that the actual phrase "recipient design" is first used, in Lecture 5 (1992, vol. 2, p. 446), which is the basis of his later article with Schegloff, "Two preferences in the organization of reference to persons in conversation and their interaction" (1979). In Lecture 4, Fall 1971, he proposes the following maxim: "A speaker should, on producing the talk he does, orient to his recipient" (1992, vol. 2, p. 438).

In a footnote after the term is introduced in SS (pp. 727, n. 40), the authors thank Garfinkel for helping them to recognize the importance of the notion of how a general principle (recipient design) can "particularize" conversational interaction.

16 For further references on these topics, see the bibliographies in Atkinson and Heritage, 1984; C. Goodwin and Heritage, 1990; Heritage, 1989; and Zimmerman, 1988.

CHAPTER 3

1 See Appendix for a discussion of the sources of the conversational data examined throughout the book.

2 The problem of reference is an important one in both linguistics and philosophy, each with voluminous literatures of their own. In philosophy, see e.g., French et al., 1979. In linguistics, see Lyons, 1977, chs 7 and 15; Nunberg, 1978; and their bibliographies for a sampling of such work.

3 The following, to the best of my knowledge, are all the places in which Sacks gave more than passing attention to the subject of pronouns: 1992, vol. 1, pp. 144 ("The use of We"); 163 ("You"); 333 ("We" (indexicals)); 348 ("You"); 382 ("Possessive pronouns"); 568 ("We" – detailed discussion of pronouns and categoricals); 610 ("Pro-terms" (mostly pro-verbs)); 701 ("Pronouns"); 730 ("Pro-verbs and

performatives"); and finally, vol. 2, p. 391 ("Agent–client interaction" on reference and pronoun choices (eg., I vs. we)).

4 Clayman (1992) uses the concept of footing to discuss shifting alignments in television news interviews. He demonstrates that inter- viewers "shift footings to display provocative viewpoints for sub- sequent topical development, to counter an interviewee and thus give voice to 'the other side' of an issue, and to generate disagreement between interviewees" (p. 196), all while appearing to maintain an institutional neutrality.

5 In a Spring 1966 lecture, Sacks (1992, vol. 1, p. 286) in fact precedes Goffman in noticing this problem when he asks, "what's the status in a multi-party conversation of persons who are not addressed by some utterance?" He asks whether they have "rights to listen in," or "a business to listen in" as members of the group. He recognizes here the involvement obligations of group members even when they are unaddressed and calls attention, at least implicitly, to the fact that the status of hearer is not a simple one.

6 Where they are relevant, I will employ Levinson's more specific terms, but since they represent a terminological rather than a conceptual improvement, I will not discuss his categories in detail. The reader is encouraged to read Levinson's very interesting essay (1988), how- ever.

7 The moral implication of this claim makes relevant the distracting interruption about integrity by David. David's three attempts to enter the talk use both a pronominal ("you") and a topical (integrity) approach to get the attention of the talkers.

8 In this connection, Liberman's (1982) discussion of Pitjantjatjara congenial meeting talk is apposite. He claims that in meetings, Pitjantjatjara men use lexical and prosodic devices to indicate their shared identity and to de-emphasize individuality. Agreement and connectedness with previous talk are prized as indicators of group affiliation. See also M. Goodwin's (1980a) discussion of the use of "Let's" as a contraction for "Let us" in directive speech. Its use "includes both speaker and hearer as potential agents of the action to be performed" (p. 166). See also T. Labov, 1980, ch. 8.2 on "The right to say we."

9 See M. Goodwin's discussion (1990) of gender differences in the use of directives, and especially "I" versus "we" in boys' talk versus girls' talk. See also the discussion of this issue in ch. 4.

10 The significance and history of the absence of the t/v (singular–plural) (*tu/vous, tu/usted, du/Sie*) distinction in English that is found in so many other Indo-European languages has been widely commented upon and analyzed in the linguistic literature. One of the earliest accounts is Brown and Gilman, 1960.

11 Mackay (1980a and b) points out how some have used the ambiguity of "they" in an attempt to resolve the problem of gender specification in third person singulars.

12 See esp. Sacks's references to this literature, 1992, vol. 1, p. 164.

CHAPTER 4

1 See M. Goodwin's (1990) discussion of the value of ethnographic work over interview research, esp. pp. 134–7 and her ch. 2 on fieldwork.

2 See Maccoby and Jacklin, 1974, for the most thorough, though by now dated, review of the psychological literature on gender. Basow, 1986, is a more current review of gender stereotypes. Baker-Miller, 1986, provides a good account of current research on the "new psychology of women."

3 Two early collections that illustrate this approach are Thorne and Henley, 1975, and Thorne et al. 1983.

4 Schegloff (1987b) is skeptical about the relation between gender and interruptions for different reasons. He points out that the gender and interruptions literature often ignores participants' own perceptions of what is going on, and that the link between gender and "specific conversational mechanisms" (p. 215) is far from "straightforward."

5 See Heise, 1979, for a discussion of transients and fundamentals.

6 This suggests an interesting speculation. If women are indeed more empathetic and sensitive to others' reactions than are men, then it is not unlikely that they might adopt the style of their interlocutor more often than men would. There is some literature on speech accommodation, especially in terms of dialect or accent shifting between ethnic groups (e.g. Franco- and Anglo-phone Canadians) (see Giles, 1979). It might be profitable to study this phenomenon in male–female conversations.

CHAPTER 5

1 See ch. 2, n. 15, for a brief history of Sacks's development of the term.

2 See esp. W. Labov and Fanshel's (1977) discussion of power relations in question-and-answer routines.

3 Schegloff (1980) points out that this routine can serve as a permission request in such nonconversational talk as interviews or doctor–patient interactions – in other words, in the more formal settings in which turn-taking is not under conversational restrictions. It is interesting to

note that this sequence ("Let me ask you a question," etc.) is overly formal for conversation, and in that way marks its other than literal interpretation.

4 Despite Heritage's (1990/1) caution about the difficulties involved in attributing intentions based on what talkers say, analysis of conventionalized strategies, such as action projections, which are recognized by both speaker and hearers to lead in a certain direction, seems to be a legitimate instance of inference about a speaker's goals. What is important is to concentrate on what the talk is doing in terms of how the talkers respond to it.

5 My thanks to Donna Eder for pointing this out to me.

6 It is not absolutely clear, without a film record, whether Rich's question is directed specifically at Amy or at the group more generally. After repeated listening to this sequence, I believe that Rich directed his query at Amy. This is because the two of them frequently engaged in dialogues within the larger conversation, and because, as film of other segments shows, the two shared a couch and were frequently oriented toward each other. It may be that Amy self-selected to answer this question, as the expert, but I think it is more likely that Rich chose her to answer.

7 Compare this with the equally choppy claim made by the doctor (lines 14–18) in the previously cited Maynard example.

CHAPTER 6

1 The concept of accounts is used in two related but distinct ways in the sociological literature. Symbolic interactionists, influenced by both Mills (1981) and Austin (1979), use "accounts" to refer to explanations or excuses, whereas ethnomethodologists use "accounting practices" or "account-ability" to refer to the assumption that social action is organized in such a way that it "makes sense," is recognizable or accountable, to its intended recipients. Austin (1979, originally 1956–7), Scott and Lyman (1968), and Hewitt and Stokes (1975) all discuss accounts as explanations, or excuses, or justifications, but make no mention of the design problems which social actors face in constructing action.

Garfinkel takes the idea of accounts and accountability further by recognizing that they must be central to a science that seeks to understand the structure of everyday activities. For Garfinkel, accounts are intended as recognizable tokens of actions, a means of producing intersubjectivity. Social actors must produce pieces of behavior which their interactants can recognize, in other words, making them accountable. "The activities whereby members produce and manage settings of organized everyday affairs are identical with members' procedures for making those settings 'accountable'" (1967, p. 1).

Heritage uses "accounts" in the ethnomethodological sense of activities designed to make sense of actions, but we can see in this instance, when he is discussing dispreferred actions or frustrations, the similarities of the two uses.

2 David Bakan (1966) makes essentially the same distinction in the psychological literature, which he refers to as communion versus agency.

3 I make this claim tentatively. It is an interesting speculation that needs further research. My thanks to Allen Grimshaw for suggesting caution here.

CHAPTER 7

1 For an interesting discussion that also recognizes the relevance of semiotics to "language in use," see Boden's discussion of "signed objects" (1994, ch. 3).

2 See the discussions of Peirce and Husserl in ch. 2 for a more elaborate presentation of these concepts.

3 For a very different sociological approach to morality that takes Mead's ideas seriously, but does not account for any of the above interactional considerations, see Schwalbe, 1991.

References

Adler, P. and Adler, P. A. 1980: Symbolic interactionism. In J. Douglas (ed.), *Introduction to the Sociologies of Everyday Life*, Boston: Allyn and Bacon, 20–61.

Alexander, C. and Wiley, M. 1981: Situated activity and identity formation. In M. Rosenberg and R. Turner (eds), *Social Psychology: Sociological Perspectives*, New York: Basic Books, 269–89.

Aries, E. 1976: Interaction patterns and themes of male, female, and mixed groups. *Small Group Behavior*, 7, 7–18.

Atkinson, P. 1988: Ethnomethodology: a critical review. *Annual Review of Sociology*, 14, 441–65.

Atkinson, P. and Heritage, J. (eds) 1984: *Structures of Social Action: Studies in Conversation Analysis*. New York: Cambridge University Press.

Austin, J. 1975: *How to Do Things with Words*. Cambridge, Mass.: Harvard University Press.

Austin, J. 1979: A plea for excuses. In J. Austin, *Philosophical Papers*, London: Oxford University Press, 175–204.

Backman, C. 1988: The self: a dialectical approach. In L. Berkowitz (ed.), *Advances in Experimental Social Psychology*, New York: Academic Press, vol. 21, 229–60.

Bakan, D. 1966: *The Duality of Human Existence*. Chicago: Rand-McNally.

Baker-Miller, S. 1986: *Toward a New Psychology of Women*, 2nd edn. Boston: Beacon Press.

Bakhtin, M. 1981: *The Dialogic Imagination*. Austin: University of Texas Press.

Bales, R. 1950: *Interaction Process Analysis*. Cambridge, Mass.: Addison-Wesley.

Basow, S. 1986: *Gender Stereotypes: Traditions and Alternatives*, 2nd edn. Pacific Grove, Calif.: Brooks/Cole.

164

Bateson, G. 1972: *Steps to an Ecology of Mind.* New York: Ballantine.

Benveniste, E. 1971: *Problems in General Linguistics.* Coral Gables, Fla.: University of Miami Press.

Berkowitz, L. 1988: Social psychological studies of the self: perspectives and programs. In *Advances in Experimental Social Psychology,* vol. 21, New York: Academic Press.

Blom, J.-P. and J. Gumperz 1972: Social meaning in linguistic structures: code-switching in Norway. In J. Gumperz and D. Hymes (eds), *Directions in Sociolinguistics,* New York: Holt, Rinehart, and Winston, 407–34.

Blumer, H. 1969: *Symbolic Interactionism: Perspective and Method.* Englewood Cliffs, NJ: Prentice-Hall.

Boden, D. 1990: People are talking: conversation analysis and symbolic interaction. In H. Becker and M. McCall (eds), *Symbolic Interaction and Cultural Studies,* Chicago: University of Chicago Press, 244–74.

Boden, D. 1994: *The Business of Talk: Organizations in Action.* Cambridge: Polity Press.

Brown, P. and Levinson, S. 1978: Universals in language usage: politeness phenomena. In E. Goody (ed.), *Questions and Politeness: Strategies in Social Interaction,* New York: Cambridge University Press, 56–289.

Brown, R. and Gilman, A. 1960: The pronouns of power and solidarity. In T. Sebeok (ed.), *Style in Language,* Cambridge, Mass.: MIT Press, 253–76.

Burling, R. 1970: *Man's Many Voices: Language in its Cultural Context.* New York: Holt, Rinehart and Winston.

Button, G. (ed.) 1991: *Ethnomethodology and the Human Sciences.* New York: Cambridge University Press.

Calhoun, C. 1991: Morality, identity, and historical explanation: Charles Taylor on the sources of the self. *Sociological Theory,* 9, 232–63.

Chafe, W. 1982: Integration and involvement in speaking, writing, and oral literature. In D. Tannen (ed.), *Spoken and Written Language,* Norwood, NJ: Ablex, 35–53.

Chodorow, N. 1978: *The Reproduction of Mothering: Psychoanalysis and the Sociology of Gender.* Berkeley: University of California Press.

Chomsky, N. 1957: *Syntactic Structures.* The Hague: Mouton.

Cicourel, A. 1974: *Cognitive Sociology.* New York: Free Press.

Clayman, S. 1992: Footing in the achievement of neutrality: the case of news-interview discourse. In P. Drew and J. Heritage (eds), *Talk at Work: Interaction in Institutional Settings,* New York: Cambridge University Press, 163–98.

Collins, R. 1989: Toward a neo-Meadian sociology of mind. *Symbolic Interaction,* 12, 1–32.

Cook-Gumperz, J. and Gumperz, J. 1976: Context in children's speech. Working paper no. 46. Language Behavior Research Laboratory: Papers on Language and Context. University of California, Berkeley.

(Repr. in N. Waterson and C. Snow (eds), *The Development of Communication*, New York: Wiley, 1978.)

Cooley, C. 1922: *Human Nature and the Social Order*. New York: Charles Scribner's Sons.

Corsaro, W. 1985: *Friendship and Peer Culture in the Early Years*. Norwood, NJ: Ablex.

Craig, R. and Tracey, K. 1983: *Conversational Coherence*. Beverly Hills, Calif.: Sage.

Davidson, P. and Costello, C. 1969: *N = 1: Experimental Studies of Single Cases*. New York: Van Nostrand Reinhold.

Dewey, J. 1896: The reflex arc concept in psychology. *Psychological Review*, 3, 357–70.

Dewey, J. 1922: *Human Nature and Conduct*. New York: Henry Holt.

Douglas, J. 1976: *Investigative Social Research*. Beverly Hills, Calif.: Sage.

Drew, P. and Wooton, A. (eds) 1988: *Erving Goffman: Exploring the Interaction Order*. Boston: Northeastern University Press.

Duranti, A. and Goodwin, C. (eds) 1992: *Rethinking Context: Language as an Interactive Phenomenon*. New York: Cambridge University Press.

Durkheim, E. 1912: *The Elementary Forms of the Religious Life*. New York: Collier.

Edelsky, C. 1993: Who's got the floor? In D. Tannen (ed.), *Gender and Conversational Interaction*, New York: Oxford University Press, 189–227.

Eder, D. 1982: The impact of management and turn allocation activities on student performance. *Discourse Processes*. 5, 147–60.

Eder, D. 1995: *School Talk: Gender and Adolescent Culture*. New Brunswick, NJ: Rutgers University Press.

Eder, D. and Hallinan, M. 1978: Sex differences in children's friendships. *American Sociological Review*, 43, 237–50.

Elias, N. 1978: *What is Sociology?* New York: Columbia University Press.

Emerson, J. 1970: Behavior in private places. In H. Dreitzel (ed.), *Recent Sociology*, no. 2, New York: Macmillan, 73–100.

Erickson, F. and Shultz, J. 1982: *The Counselor as Gatekeeper*. New York: Academic Press.

Fairbairn, W. 1952: *An Object-Relations Theory of the Personality*. New York: Basic Books.

Fehr, B. and Stetson, J. 1990: A bibliography for ethnomethodology. In J. Coulter (ed.), *Ethnomethodological Sociology*, Brookfield, Vt: Edward Elgar, 473–559.

Fine, G. 1993: The sad demise, mysterious disappearance, and glorious triumph of symbolic interactionism. *Annual Review of Sociology*, 19, 61–87.

Fisher, S. 1982: The decision making context: how doctors and patients communicate. In R. DiPietro (ed.), *Linguistics and the Professions*, Norwood, NJ: Ablex, 51–81.

Fishman, P. 1978: Interaction: the work women do. *Social Problems*, 25, 397–406.

French, P., Uehling, T. Jr. and Wettstein, H. 1979: *Contemporary Perspectives in the Philosophy of Language*. Minneapolis: University of Minnesota Press.

Gallant, M. and Kleinman, S. 1983: Symbolic interactionism vs. ethnomethodology. *Symbolic Interaction*, 6, 1–18.

Gallant, M. and Kleinman, S. 1985: Making sense of interpretations: response to Rawls on the debate between symbolic interactionism and ethnomethodology. *Symbolic Interaction*, 8, 141–5.

Gallie, W. 1966: *Peirce and Pragmatism*. New York: Dover.

Garfinkel, H. 1963: A conception of, and experiments with, "trust" as a condition of stable concerted actions. In O. Harvey (ed.), *Motivation and Social Interaction*, New York: Ronald Press, 187–238.

Garfinkel, H. 1967: *Studies in Ethnomethodology*. Englewood Cliffs, NJ: Prentice-Hall.

Garfinkel, H. 1974: On the origins of the term "ethnomethodology". In R. Turner (ed.), *Ethnomethodology*, Harmondsworth: Penguin, 15–18.

Garfinkel, H. and Sacks, H. 1970: On formal structures of practical actions. In J. McKinney and E. Tiryakian (eds), *Theoretical Sociology*, New York: Appleton-Century-Crofts, 338–66.

Geertz, C. 1973: Thick description: toward an interpretive theory of culture. In C. Geertz, *The Interpretation of Cultures*, New York: Basic Books, 3–30.

Geertz, C. 1983: *Local Knowledge: Further Essays in Interpretive Anthropology*. New York: Basic Books.

Gergen, K. 1991: *The Saturated Self: Dilemmas of Identity in Contemporary Life*. New York: Basic Books.

Giddens, A. 1979: *Central Problems in Social Theory*. Berkeley: University of California Press.

Giddens, A. 1984: *The Constitution of Society*. Berkeley: University of California Press.

Giddens, A. 1988: Goffman as a systematic social theorist. In P. Drew and A. Wooton (eds), *Erving Goffman: Exploring the Interaction Order*, Boston: Northeastern University Press, 250–79.

Giles, H. 1979: Ethnicity markers in speech. In K. Scherer and H. Giles (eds), *Social Markers in Speech*, New York: Cambridge University Press, 251–91.

Gill, V. and Maynard, D. 1995: On "labeling" in actual interaction: delivering and receiving diagnoses of developmental disabilities. *Social Problems*, 42, 11–37.

167

Gilligan, C. 1979: Woman's place in man's life cycle. *Harvard Educational Review*, 49, 31–45.

Gilligan, C. 1982: *In a Different Voice: Psychological Theory and Women's Development*. Cambridge, Mass.: Harvard University Press.

Gleason, J. and Greif, E. 1983: Men's speech to young children. In B. Thorne, C. Kramarae, and N. Henley (eds), *Language, Gender and Society*, Rowley, Mass.: Newbury House, 140–50.

Goffman, E. 1953: Communication conduct in an island community. Ph.D. diss., University of Chicago.

Goffman, E. 1959: *The Presentation of Self in Everyday Life*. New York: Doubleday.

Goffman, E. 1961a: *Asylums*. New York: Doubleday.

Goffman, E. 1961b: *Encounters: Two Studies in the Sociology of Interaction*. Indianapolis: Bobbs-Merrill.

Goffman, E. 1963a: *Behavior in Public Places*. New York: Free Press.

Goffman, E. 1963b: *Stigma*. Englewood Cliffs, NJ: Prentice-Hall.

Goffman, E. 1964: The neglected situation. *American Anthropologist*, 66 (part II, special issue), 133–6.

Goffman, E. 1967: *Interaction Ritual*. New York: Doubleday.

Goffman, E. 1969: *Strategic Interaction: An Analysis of Doubt and Calculation in Face-to-Face, Day-to-Day Dealings with One Another*. New York: Ballantine Books.

Goffman, E. 1971: *Relations in Public*. New York: Harper and Row.

Goffman, E. 1974: *Frame Analysis*. New York: Harper and Row.

Goffman, E. 1976: Gender display. *Studies in the Anthropology of Visual Communication*, 3, 69–77.

Goffman, E. 1981: *Forms of Talk*. Philadelphia: University of Pennsylvania Press.

Goffman, E. 1983a: Felicity's condition. *American Journal of Sociology*, 89, 1–53.

Goffman, E. 1983b: Presidential address: the interaction order. *American Sociological Review*, 48, 1–17.

Goodwin, C. 1981: *Conversational Organization: Interaction Between Speakers and Hearers*. New York: Academic Press.

Goodwin, C. and Heritage, J. 1990: Conversation analysis. *Annual Review of Anthropology*, 19, 283–307.

Goodwin, M. 1980a: Directive-response speech sequences in girls' and boys' task activities. In S. McConnell-Ginet, R. Borker, and N. Furman (eds), *Women and Language in Literature and Society*, New York: Praeger, 157–73.

Goodwin, M. 1980b: He-said-she-said: formal cultural procedures for the construction of a gossip dispute activity. *American Ethnologist*, 7, 674–95.

Goodwin, M. 1990: *He-Said-She-Said: Talk as Social Organization among Black Children*. Bloomington: Indiana University Press.

Goodwin, M. 1993: Tactical uses of stories: participation frameworks within boys' and girls' disputes. In D. Tannen (ed.), *Gender and Conversational Interaction*, New York: Oxford University Press, 110–43.

Goody, E. 1978: Towards a theory of questions. In E. Goody (ed.), *Questions and Politeness: Strategies in Social Interaction*, New York: Cambridge University Press, 17–43.

Gouldner, A. 1970: *The Coming Crisis of Western Sociology*. New York: Basic Books.

Grimes, J. 1975: *The Thread of Discourse*. New York: Mouton.

Grimshaw, A. 1980: Selection and labeling of instrumentalities of verbal manipulation. *Discourse Processes*, 3, 203–29.

Grimshaw, A. 1981: Talk and social control. In A. Grimshaw (ed.), *Language as Social Resource*, Palo Alto, Calif.: Stanford University Press, 265–320. (Also in M. Rosenberg and R. Turner (eds), *Social Psychology: Sociological Perspectives*, New York: Basic Books, 200–32.)

Grimshaw, A. 1989: *Collegial Discourse: Professional Conversation among Peers*. Norwood, NJ: Ablex.

Grimshaw, A. (ed.) 1994: *What's Going on Here? Complementary Studies of Professional Talk* (vol. 2 of the Multiple Analysis Project). Norwood, NJ: Ablex.

Gumperz, J. 1982: *Discourse Strategies*. New York: Cambridge University Press.

Halliday, M. 1978: *Language as Social Semiotic: The Social Interpretation of Language and Meaning*. Baltimore: University Park Press.

Heise, D. 1979: *Understanding Events*. New York: Cambridge University Press.

Heritage, J. 1983: Accounts in action. In G. Gilbert and P. Abell (eds), *Accounts and Action*, Aldershot: Gower, 117–31.

Heritage, J. 1984: *Garfinkel and Ethnomethodology*. Cambridge: Polity Press.

Heritage, J. 1989: Current developments in conversation analysis. In D. Roger and P. Bull (eds), *Conversation: An Interdisciplinary Perspective*, Clevedon: Multilingual Matters, 21–47.

Heritage, J. 1990/1: Intention, meaning and strategy: observations on constraints on interaction analysis. *Research on Language and Social Interaction*, 24, 311–32.

Heritage, J. and Watson, D. 1980: Aspects of the properties of formulations in natural conversations: some instances analyzed. *Semiotica*, 30, 245–62.

Hewitt, J. 1988: *Self and Society: A Symbolic Interactionist Social Psychology*. 2nd edn. Boston: Allyn and Bacon.

Hewitt, J. and Stokes, R. 1975: Disclaimers. *American Sociological Review*, 40, 1–11.

Hilbert, R. 1992: *The Classical Roots of Ethnomethodology: Durkheim, Weber, and Garfinkel.* Chapel Hill: University of North Carolina Press.

Homans, G. 1950: *The Human Group.* New York: Harcourt, Brace, and World.

Hughes, E. 1945: Dilemmas and contradictions of status. *American Journal of Sociology*, 50, 353–9.

Husserl, E. 1960: *Cartesian Meditations*, trans. D. Cairns. The Hague: Mouton. (Orig. pub. in 1931.)

Husserl, E. 1965: Philosophy as rigorous science. In E. Husserl, *Phenomenology and the Crisis of Philosophy*, trans. Q. Lauer, New York: Harper and Row (Orig. pub. in *Logos* I. (1911): 289–341).

Husserl, E. 1970: *Logical Investigations*, trans J. Findlay. Atlantic Heights, NJ. Humanities Press. (Orig. pub. in 1901.)

Husserl, E. 1981a: Husserl's inaugural lecture at Freiburg im Breisgau (1917). In P. McCormick and F. Elliston (eds), *Husserl: Shorter Works*, Notre Dame, Ind.: University of Notre Dame Press, 9–17.

Husserl, E. 1981b: Phenomenology. In P. McCormick and F. Elliston (eds), *Husserl: Shorter Works*, Notre Dame, Ind.: University of Notre Dame Press, 21–35. (Revised translation by R. Palmer of Husserl's 1929 article for the 14th edn of *The Encyclopaedia Britannica*.)

Jakobson, R. 1957: *Shifters, Verbal Categories, and the Russian Verb.* Cambridge, Mass.: Harvard University Russian Language Project.

Jakobson, R., Fant, C. and Halle, M. 1952: *Preliminaries to Speech Analysis*, 2nd edn. Cambridge, Mass.: MIT Press.

James, D. and Clarke, S. 1993: Women, men, and interruptions: a critical review. In D. Tannen (ed.), *Gender and Conversational Interaction*, New York: Oxford University Press, 231–80.

James, W. 1981: The social self. In G. Stone and H. Farberman (eds), *Social Psychology through Symbolic Interaction*, New York: John Wiley and Sons, 163–7. (Orig. pub. in 1892 in *Psychology*, New York: Henry Holt.)

Jefferson, G. 1974: Error correction as an interactional resource. *Language in Society*, 2, 181–99.

Jefferson, G. 1978: Sequential aspects of story telling in conversation. In J. Schenkein (ed.), *Studies in the Organization of Conversational Interaction*, New York: Academic Press, 219–48.

Jefferson, G. 1979: A technique for inviting laughter and its subsequent acceptance/declination. In G. Psathas (ed.), *Everyday Language*, New York: Irvington, 79–96.

Johnstone, B. 1993: Community and contest: Midwestern men and women creating their worlds in conversational storytelling. In D. Tannen (ed.), *Gender and Conversational Interaction*, New York: Oxford University Press, 62–80.

Keenan, E. and Schieffelin, B. 1976: Topic as a discourse notion: a study of topic in the conversation of children and adults. In C. N. Li (ed.), *Subject and Topic*, New York: Academic Press, 335–84.

Kendon, A. 1988: Goffman's approach to face-to-face interaction. In P. Drew and A. Wooton (eds), *Erving Goffman: Exploring the Interaction Order*, Boston: Northeastern University Press, 14–40.

Kendon, A. 1990: *Conducting Interaction: Patterns of Behavior in Focused Encounters*. New York: Cambridge University Press.

Kerby, A. 1991: *Narrative and the SELF*. Bloomington: Indiana University Press.

Kohlberg, L. 1981: *The Philosophy of Moral Development*. New York: Harper and Row.

Laberge, S. and Sankoff, G. 1980: Anything you can do. In G. Sankoff (ed.), *The Social Life of Language*, New York: Academic Press, 271–93.

Labov, T. 1980: The appearance of moral matters in talk: a study of verbal interaction in a food cooperative. Ph.D. diss., Department of Sociology, Columbia University.

Labov, T. 1994: Discussion. In A. Grimshaw (ed.), *What's Going on Here? Complementary Studies of Professional Talk* (vol. 2 of the Multiple Analysis Project), Norwood, NJ: Ablex, 368–71.

Labov, W. and Fanshel, D. 1977: *Therapeutic Discourse: Psychotherapy as Conversation*. New York: Academic Press.

Labov, W. and Waletsky, J. 1967: Narrative analysis: oral versions of personal experience. In J. Helm (ed.), *Essays on the Verbal and Visual Arts*, Seattle: University of Washington Press, 12–44.

Lakoff, R. 1975: *Language and Woman's Place*. New York: Harper's.

Lakoff, R. 1977: Women's language. *Language and Style: An International Journal*, 10, 222–47.

Lemert, C. 1994: Dark thoughts about the self. In C. Calhoun (ed.), *Social Theory and the Politics of Identity*, Oxford: Blackwell, 100–29.

Lerner, G. 1991: On the syntax of sentences-in-progress. *Language in Society*, 20, 441–58.

Lever, J. 1978: Sex differences in the complexity of children's play and games. *American Sociological Review*, 43, 471–83.

Levinson, S. 1983: *Pragmatics*. New York: Cambridge University Press.

Levinson, S. 1988: Putting linguistics on a proper footing: explorations in Goffman's concepts of participation. In P. Drew and A. Wooton (eds), *Erving Goffman: Exploring the Interaction Order*, Boston: Northeastern University Press, 161–227.

Liberman, K. 1982: Some linguistic features of congenial fellowship among the Pitjantjatjara. *International Journal of the Sociology of Language*, 36, 35–51.

Lipman-Blumen, J. 1984: *Gender Roles and Power*. Englewood Cliffs, NJ: Prentice-Hall.

Luckmann, T. 1978: Preface to T. Luckmann (ed.), *Phenomenology and Sociology: Selected Readings*, Harmondsworth: Penguin, 7–13.

Lyons, J. 1968: *Theoretical Linguistics*. New York: Cambridge University Press.

Lyons, J. 1977: *Semantics*. New York: Cambridge University Press.

Maccoby, E. and Jacklin, C. 1974: *The Psychology of Sex Differences*. Palo Alto, Calif.: Stanford University Press.

Mackay, D. 1980a: On the goals, principles, and procedures for prescriptive grammar: singular they. *Language in Society*, 9, 349–67.

Mackay, D. 1980b: Psychology, prescriptive grammar and the pronoun problem. *American Psychologist*, 35, 444–9.

Malinowski, B. 1959: The problem of meaning in primitive languages. In C. Ogden and I. Richards (eds), *The Meaning of Meaning*, New York: Harcourt, Brace and World, 296–336.

Malone, M. 1985: Speech and social identity: sociolinguistic patterns and identity presentation. Ph.D. diss., Department of Sociology, Indiana University.

Malone, M. 1994: Small disagreements: character contests and working consensus in informal talk. *Symbolic Interaction*, 17, 107–27.

Malone, M. 1995: How to do things with friends: altercasting and recipient design. *Research on Language and Social Interaction*, 28, 147–70.

Malone, M. 1996: Semiotics. In D. Levinson and M. Ember (eds), *The Encyclopedia of Cultural Anthropology*, Lakeville, Conn.: American Reference, 1150–4.

Maltz, D. and Borker, R. 1982: A cultural approach to male–female miscommunication. In J. Gumperz (ed.), *Language and Social Identity*, New York: Cambridge University Press, 196–216.

Mandelbaum, J. 1990/1: Beyond mundane reason: conversation analysis and context. *Research on Language and Social Interaction*, 24, 333–50.

Mannheim, K. 1971: On the interpretation of *Weltanschauung*. In K. Mannheim, *From Karl Mannheim*, New York: Oxford University Press, 8–58.

Maynard, D. 1989: Perspective display sequences in conversation. *Western Journal of Speech Communication*, 53, 91–113.

Maynard, D. 1991a: Interaction and asymmetry in clinical discourse. *American Journal of Sociology*, 97, 448–95.

Maynard, D. 1991b: The perspective-display series and the delivery and receipt of diagnostic news. In D. Boden and D. H. Zimmerman (eds), *Talk and Social Structure: Studies in Ethnomethodology and Conversation Analysis*, Cambridge: Polity, 164–92.

Maynard, D. 1992: On clinicians co-implicating recipients' perspective in the delivery of diagnostic news. In P. Drew and J. Heritage (eds), *Talk at Work: Social Interaction in Institutional Settings*, New York: Cambridge University Press, 331–58.

Mead, G. H. 1932: *The Philosophy of the Present*. Chicago: University of Chicago Press.

Mead, G. H. 1934: *Mind, Self, and Society from the Standpoint of a Social Behaviorist*. Chicago: University of Chicago Press.

Mead, G. H. 1936: *Movements of Thought in the Nineteenth Century*. Chicago: University of Chicago Press.

Mead, G. H. 1938: *The Philosophy of the Act*. Chicago: University of Chicago Press.

Mead, G. H. 1964: *Selected Writings*, ed. A. Reck. Chicago: University of Chicago Press.

Mehan, H. 1979: *Learning Lessons*. Cambridge, Mass.: Harvard University Press.

Meltzer, B., Petras, J. and Reynolds, L. 1975: *Symbolic Interactionism: Genesis, Varieties, and Criticism*. Boston: Routledge and Kegan Paul.

Miller, D. 1973: *George Herbert Mead: Self, Language, and the World*. Chicago: University of Chicago Press.

Mills, C. 1981: Situated actions and vocabularies of motive. In J. Stone and H. Farberman (eds), *Social Psychology through Symbolic Interaction*, New York: John Wiley and Sons, 325–33. (Orig. pub. in 1940 in *American Sociological Review*, 5, 904–13.)

Nunberg, G. 1978: *The Pragmatics of Reference*. Bloomington: Indiana University Linguistics Club.

O'Barr, W. 1982: *Linguistic Evidence*. New York: Academic Press.

Ochs, E. 1979: Planned and unplanned discourse. In T. Givon (ed.), *Syntax and Semantics, Vol. 12: Discourse and Syntax*, New York: Academic Press, 51–80.

Ochs, E. 1992: Indexing gender. In A. Duranti and C. Goodwin (eds), *Rethinking Context: Language as an Interactive Phenomenon*, New York: Cambridge University Press, 335–58.

Olson, D. 1977: From utterance to text: the bias of language in speech and writing. *Harvard Education Review*, 47, 257–81.

Peirce, C. 1931–58: *Collected Papers*, vols 1–6, ed. C. Hartshorne and P. Weiss, vols 7–8, ed. A. Burks. Cambridge, Mass.: Harvard University Press.

Peirce, C. 1982–92: *Writings of Charles S. Peirce: A Chronological Edition*, vols 1–5 (15 vols projected). Bloomington: Indiana University Press.

Perinbanayagam, R. 1991: *Discursive Acts*. New York: Aldine de Gruyter.

Petras, J. (ed.) 1968: *George Herbert Mead: Essays on His Social Philosophy*. New York: Teachers' College Press.

Philipsen, G. 1975: Speaking like a "man" in Teamsterville: culture patterns of role enactment in an urban neighborhood. *Quarterly Journal of Speech*, 61, 12–22.

Pleck, J. 1981: *The Myth of Masculinity*. Cambridge, Mass.: MIT Press.

173

Pomerantz, A. 1984a: Agreeing and disagreeing with assessments: some features of preferred and dispreferred turn shapes. In J. Atkinson and J. Heritage (eds), *Structures of Social Action: Studies in Conversation Analysis*, New York: Cambridge University Press, 57–101.

Pomerantz, A. 1984b: Pursuing a response. In J. Atkinson and J. Heritage (eds), *Structures of Social Action: Studies in Conversation Analysis*, New York: Cambridge University Press, 152–63.

Rawls, A. 1984: Interaction as a resource for epistemological critique. *Sociological Theory*, 2, 222–52.

Rawls, A. 1985: Reply to Gallant and Kleinman on symbolic interactionism vs. ethnomethodology. *Symbolic Interaction*, 8, 121–40.

Rawls, A. 1987: The interaction order *sui generis*: Goffman's contribution to social theory. *Sociological Theory*, 5, 136–49.

Rawls, A. 1989a: An ethnomethodological perspective on social theory. In D. Helm et al. (eds), *The Interactional Order*, New York: Irvington, 4–20.

Rawls, A. 1989b: Language, self, and social order: a reformulation of Goffman and Sacks. *Human Studies*, 12, 147–92.

Rawls, A. 1990: Emergent sociality: a dialectic of commitment and order. *Symbolic Interaction*, 13, 63–82.

Ricoeur, P. 1970: *Freud and Philosophy: An Essay on Interpretation*. New Haven: Yale University Press.

Ricoeur, P. 1981: *Hermeneutics and the Human Sciences*, ed. and trans. J. Thompson. New York: Cambridge University Press.

Roberts, J. and Sutton-Smith, B. 1962: Child training and game involvement. *Ethnology*, 1, 166–85.

Rubin, L. 1983: *Intimate Strangers: Men and Women Together*. New York: Harper and Row.

Sacks, H. 1963: Sociological description. *Berkeley Journal of Sociology*, 8, 1–16.

Sacks, H. 1964: Unpublished lectures, Irvine: University of California. (Cited in Rawls, 1989a.)

Sacks, H. 1972: On the analyzability of stories by children. In J. Gumperz and D. Hymes (eds), *Directions in Sociolinguistics*, New York: Holt, Rinehart, and Winston, 325–45.

Sacks, H. 1974: An analysis of the course of a joke's telling in conversation. In R. Bauman and J. Sherzer (eds), *Explorations in the Ethnography of Speaking*, New York: Cambridge University Press, 337–53.

Sacks, H. 1984: Notes on methodology. In J. Atkinson and J. Heritage (eds), *Structures of Social Action: Studies in Conversation Analysis*, New York: Cambridge University Press, 21–7.

Sacks, H. 1992: *Lectures on Conversation*, vols 1 and 2, ed. G. Jefferson. Cambridge, Mass.: Blackwell.

Sacks, H., Schegloff, E. and Jefferson, G. 1974: A simplest systematics for the organization of turn taking for conversation. *Language*, 50,

696–735. (Repr. in J. Schenkein (ed.), 1978 *Studies in the Organization of Conversational Interaction*, New York: Academic Press, 7–55.)

Sanders, R. 1991: The two-way relationship between talk in social interactions and actors' goals and plans. In K. Tracy (ed.), *Understanding Face-to-Face Interaction: Issues Linking Goals and Discourse*, Hillsdale, NJ: Lawrence Erlbaum Associates, 167–88.

Saussure, F. 1959: *Course in General Linguistics*, trans. with an introduction by Wade Baskin. New York: McGraw-Hill (Orig. pub. in 1915.)

Schegloff, E. 1968: Sequencing in conversational openings. *American Anthropologist*, 70, 1075–95. (Repr. in J. Gumperz and D. Hymes (eds), *Directions in Sociolinguistics*, New York: Holt, Rinehart, and Winston, 346–80.)

Schegloff, E. 1980: Preliminaries to preliminaries: can I ask you a question? *Sociological Inquiry*, 50, 104–52.

Schegloff, E. 1987a: Analyzing single episodes of interaction: an exercise in conversation analysis. *Social Psychology Quarterly*, 50, 101–14.

Schegloff, E. 1987b: Between micro and macro: contexts and other connections. In J. Alexander, B. Geisen, R. Munch and N. Smelser (eds), *The Micro–Macro Link*, Berkeley: University of California Press, 207–34.

Schegloff, E. and Sacks, H. 1974: Opening up closings. In R. Turner (ed.), *Ethnomethodology: Selected Readings*, Harmondsworth: Penguin, 233–64.

Schegloff, E., Jefferson, G. and Sacks, H. 1977: The preference for self correction in the organization of repair in conversation. *Language*, 53, 361–82.

Schenkein, J. 1978. *Studies in the Organization of Conversational Interaction*. New York: Academic Press.

Schiffrin, D. 1985: Everyday argument: the organization of diversity in talk. In T. van Dijk (ed.), *The Handbook of Discourse Analysis*, London: Academic Press, vol. 3, 35–46.

Schiffrin, D. 1987: *Discourse Markers*. New York: Cambridge University Press.

Schmitt, R. 1967: Phenomenology. In P. Edwards (ed.), *The Encyclopedia of Philosophy*, New York: Macmillan and the Free Press, vol. 6, 135–51.

Schutz, A. 1962: *Collected Papers I: The Problem of Social Reality*. The Hague: Nijhoff.

Schutz, A. 1964: *Collected Papers II: Studies in Social Theory*. The Hague: Nijhoff.

Schutz, A. 1966: *Collected Papers III: Studies in Phenomenological Philosophy*. The Hague: Nijhoff.

Schutz, A. 1967: *The Phenomenology of the Social World*, trans. G. Walsh and F. Lehnert. Evanston, Ill.: Northwestern University Press.

Schutz, A. 1970: *On Phenomenology and Social Relations,* ed. with an introduction by H. Wagner. Chicago: University of Chicago Press.

Schutz, A. and Luckmann, T. 1973: *The Structures of the Life-World.* Evanston, Ill.: Northwestern University Press.

Schwalbe, M. 1983: Language and the self: from a symbolic interactionist perspective. *Symbolic Interaction,* 6, 291–306.

Schwalbe, M. 1991: Social structure and the moral self. In J. Howard and P. Callero (eds), *The Self–Society Dynamic: Cognition, Emotion, and Action,* New York: Cambridge University Press, 281–303.

Scott, M. and Lyman, S. 1968: Accounts. *American Sociological Review,* 33, 46–62.

Sharrock, W. and Anderson, B. 1986: *The Ethnomethodologists.* New York: Tavistock.

Silverstein, M. 1976: Shifters, linguistic categories, and cultural description. In K. Basso and H. Selby (eds), *Meaning in Anthropology,* Albuquerque: University of New Mexico Press, 11–55.

Simmel, Georg 1950: *The Sociology of Georg Simmel.* New York: Free Press.

Smith, A. 1976: *The Theory of Moral Sentiments.* Oxford: Clarendon Press (Orig. pub. in 1759.)

Snyder, M. 1974: Self-monitoring of expressive behavior. *Journal of Personality and Social Psychology,* 30, 526–37.

Spiegelberg, H. 1973: On the right to say "we": a linguistic and phenomenological analysis. In G. Psathas (ed.), *Phenomenological Sociology: Issues and Applications,* New York: John Wiley and Sons, 129–56.

Stokes, R. and Hewitt, J. 1976: Aligning actions. *American Sociological Review,* 41, 838–49.

Stone, G. and Farberman, H. 1981: *Social Psychology through Symbolic Interaction.* New York: John Wiley and Sons.

Stryker, S. 1980: *Symbolic Interactionism: A Social Structural Version.* Menlo Park, Calif.: Benjamin/Cummings.

Stubbs, M. 1983: *Discourse Analysis: The Sociolinguistic Analysis of Natural Language.* Chicago: University of Chicago Press.

Sudnow, D. (ed.) 1972: *Studies in Social Interaction.* New York: Free Press.

Tannen, D. 1982: Ethnic style in male–female conversation. In J. Gumperz (ed.), *Language and Social Identity,* New York: Cambridge University Press, 217–31.

Tannen, D. 1984: *Conversational Style: Analyzing Talk Among Friends.* Norwood, NJ: Ablex.

Tannen, D. 1985: Relative focus on involvement in oral and written discourse. In D. Olson, N. Torrance, and A. Hildyard (eds), *Literacy, Language and Learning: The Nature and Consequences of Reading and Writing,* New York: Cambridge University Press, 124–47.

Tannen, D. 1990: *You Just Don't Understand: Women and Men in Conversation.* New York: Ballantine Books.

Tannen, D. (ed.) 1993: *Gender and Conversational Interaction.* New York: Oxford University Press.

Tavris, C. and Wade, C. 1984: *The Longest War: Sex Differences in Perspective.* New York: Harcourt, Brace, Jovanovich.

Taylor, C. 1989: *Sources of the Self: The Making of the Modern Identity.* Cambridge, Mass.: Harvard University Press.

Thayer, H. 1967: Pragmatism. In P. Edwards (ed.), *The Encyclopedia of Philosophy,* New York: Macmillan and the Free Press, vol. 6, 430–6.

Thomas, W. 1937: *Primitive Behavior.* New York: McGraw-Hill.

Thorne, B. 1986: Girls and boys together . . . but mostly apart: gender arrangements in elementary school. In W. Hartup and Z. Rubin (eds), *Relationships and Development,* Hillsdale, NJ: Lawrence Erlbaum Associates, 167–84.

Thorne, B. and Henley, N. (eds) 1975: *Language and Sex: Difference and Dominance.* Rowley, Mass.: Newbury House.

Thorne, B., Kramarae, C. and Henley, N. (eds) 1983: *Language, Gender and Society,* Rowley, Mass.: Newbury House.

Tipper, M. and Malone, M. 1995: Conflicting demands in writing response groups. *The Writing Instructor,* 14, 77–88.

Turner, R. 1962: Role-taking: process versus conformity. In A. Rose (ed.), *Human Nature and Social Processes,* Boston: Houghton Mifflin, 20–40.

Urban, G. 1989: The "I" of discourse. In B. Lee and G. Urban (eds), *Semiotics, Self and Society,* New York: Mouton, 27–51.

Watson, D. 1987: Interdisciplinary considerations in the analysis of pro-terms. In G. Button and J. Lee (eds), *Talk and Social Organization,* Philadelphia: Multilingual Matters, 261–89.

Weinstein, E. 1969: The development of interpersonal competence. In D. Goslin (ed.), *Handbook of Socialization Theory and Research,* Chicago: Rand-McNally, 753–75.

Weinstein, E. and Deutschberger, P. 1963: Some dimensions of altercasting. *Sociometry,* 26, 454–66.

West, C. and Fenstermaker, S. 1995: Doing difference. *Gender & Society,* 9, 8–37.

West, C. and Zimmerman, D. 1987: Doing gender. *Gender & Society,* 1, 125–51.

Wilson, T. 1991: Social structure and the sequential organization of interaction. In D. Boden and D. Zimmerman (eds), *Talk and Social Structure: Studies in Ethnomethodology and Conversation Analysis,* Cambridge, Polity, 22–43.

Wittgenstein, L. 1953: *Philosophical Investigations.* Oxford: Blackwell.

Wittgenstein, L. 1958: *The Blue and the Brown Books.* Oxford: Blackwell.

177

Zeitlin, I. 1973: *Rethinking Sociology.* New York: Appleton-Century-Crofts.

Zimmerman, D. 1988: On conversation: the conversation analytic perspective. In *Communication Yearbook II*, Newbury Park, Calif.: Sage, 406–32.

Zimmerman, D. and West, C. 1975: Sex roles, interruptions and silences in conversation. In B. Thorne and N. Henley (eds), *Language and Sex: Difference and Dominance*, Rowley, Mass.: Newbury House, 105–29.

Index